NO FEAR SHAKESPEARE

NO FEAR SHAKESPEARE

As You Like It

The Comedy of Errors

Hamlet

Henry IV, Parts One and Two

Henry V

Julius Caesar

King Lear

Macbeth

The Merchant of Venice

A Midsummer Night's Dream

Much Ado About Nothing

Othello

Richard III

Romeo and Juliet

Sonnets

The Taming of the Shrew

The Tempest

Twelfth Night

NO FEAR SHAKESPEARE

SONNETS

SPARKNOTES is a registered trademark of SparkNotes LLC

The original text and translation for this edition were prepared by John Crowther.

Spark Publishing
120 Fifth Avenue
New York, NY 10011
www.sparknotes.com

Please submit all comments and questions or report errors to *www.sparknotes.com/errors*

10 11 SN 15 14 13 12 11

Printed and bound in the United States

ISBN-13: 978-1-4114-0219-5
ISBN-10: 1-4114-0219-7

Library of Congress Cataloging-in-Publication Data

Shakespeare, William, 1564–1616.

  Sonnets / [edited by John Crowther].

      p. cm. — (No fear Shakespeare)

  ISBN 1-4114-0219-7

  1. Sonnets, English. I. Crowther, John (John C.) II. Title.

PR2848.A2C76 2004
821'.3—dc22

                            2004015832

There's matter in these sighs, these profound heaves.
You must translate: 'tis fit we understand them.

(Hamlet, 4.1.1–2)

FEAR NOT.

Have you ever found yourself looking at a Shakespeare play, then down at the footnotes, then back at the play, and still not understanding? You know what the individual words mean, but they don't add up. SparkNotes' *No Fear Shakespeare* will help you break through all that. Put the pieces together with our easy-to-read translations. Soon you'll be reading Shakespeare's own words fearlessly—and actually enjoying it.

No Fear Shakespeare puts Shakespeare's language side-by-side with a facing-page translation into modern English—the kind of English people actually speak today. When Shakespeare's words make your head spin, our translation will help you sort out what's happening, who's saying what, and why.

ORIGINAL DEDICATION

TO. THE. ONLY. BEGETTER. OF.

THESE. ENSUING. SONNETS.

Mr. W.H. ALL HAPPINESS.

AND. THAT. ETERNITY.

PROMISED.

BY.

OUR. EVER-LASTING. POET.

WISHETH.

THE. WELL-WISHING.

ADVENTURER. IN.

SETTING.

FORTH.

T.T.

The capital letters and the periods after every word may have been intended to make the dedication resemble an ancient Roman inscription in stone, suggesting that the sonnets are meant to last forever. The idea that the sonnets will outlast stone monuments and inscriptions recurs throughout the sonnets.

In publishing these sonnets, the publisher, Thomas Thorpe, wishes the man who inspired them, Mr. W. H., to receive the happiness and eternal fame promised him by the immortal poet who wrote them.

The identity of Mr. W.H. is unknown. The initials could simply be a misprint for W.Sh. (William Shakespeare), or they could refer to the person who inspired the sonnets— possibly the young man the sonnets refer to. The most popular guesses regarding the young man's identity are Henry Wriothesly, earl of Southampton, and William Herbert, earl of Pembroke.

1

From fairest creatures we desire increase,
That thereby beauty's rose might never die,
But as the riper should by time decease
His tender heir might bear his memory.
But thou, contracted to thine own bright eyes,
Feed'st thy light's flame with self-substantial fuel,
Making a famine where abundance lies,
Thyself thy foe, to thy sweet self too cruel.
Thou that art now the world's fresh ornament
And only herald to the gaudy spring,
Within thine own bud buriest thy content,
And, tender churl, mak'st waste in niggarding.
  Pity the world, or else this glutton be,
  To eat the world's due, by the grave and thee.

1

We want the most beautiful people to have children, so their beauty will be preserved forever—when the parent dies, the child he leaves behind will remind us of his beauty. But you, in love with your own pretty eyes, are letting your beauty burn itself out. You're starving the world of your beauty rather than spreading the wealth around. You're acting like your own worst enemy! Right now you're the best-looking thing in the world, the only person as beautiful as springtime. But your beauty is like a new bud, and you're letting it die before it can develop and bring you true happiness. You're a young man, but you act like an old miser—you're wasting your beauty by hoarding it and keeping it to yourself! Take pity on the rest of us, or this is how you'll be remembered: as the greedy pig who hogged his own beauty and took it with him to the grave.

2

When forty winters shall besiege thy brow
And dig deep trenches in thy beauty's field,
Thy youth's proud livery, so gazed on now,
Will be a tattered weed, of small worth held.
Then being asked where all thy beauty lies,
Where all the treasure of thy lusty days,
To say within thine own deep-sunken eyes
Were an all-eating shame and thriftless praise.
How much more praise deserved thy beauty's use
If thou couldst answer, "This fair child of mine
Shall sum my count and make my old excuse,"
Proving his beauty by succession thine.
    This were to be new made when thou art old,
    And see thy blood warm when thou feel'st it cold.

2

When forty years have gone by and carved deep wrinkles in your forehead, your youthful beauty, which everyone likes to look at now, will be worth little. Then, when someone asks you where all your beauty is—all the treasure of your virile youth—if you were to say that it's all there in your withered face and sunken eyes, that would be an all-consuming shame and nothing to be proud of. You'd have a much better excuse if, decades from now, you could say you spent your beauty and youth raising a child. If someone were to ask you why you looked so old, you could say, "The effort I spent raising this beautiful child explains the sorry old state I'm in"—and meanwhile your child's beauty would be a new incarnation of your own! Having a beautiful child would be like being born again in old age, with the blood that flows coldly in your old veins becoming warm again in his.

3

Look in thy glass and tell the face thou viewest,
Now is the time that face should form another,
Whose fresh repair if now thou not renewest,
Thou dost beguile the world, unbless some mother.
For where is she so fair whose uneared womb
Disdains the tillage of thy husbandry?
Or who is he so fond will be the tomb
Of his self-love, to stop posterity?
Thou art thy mother's glass, and she in thee
Calls back the lovely April of her prime;
So thou through windows of thine age shalt see,
Despite of wrinkles, this thy golden time.
  But if thou live remembered not to be,
  Die single and thine image dies with thee.

3

Look in your mirror and tell the face you see that it's time to father a child. Your face is fresh and healthy now, but if you don't reproduce it, you'll be cheating the world and cursing a woman who would happily be your child's mother. After all, do you think there's a woman out there so beautiful that she'd refuse to have your child? And what man would be so foolish as to allow his own self-absorption to stop himself from fathering children? You are like a mirror to your own mother, and when she looks at you she can gaze back at the lovely springtime of her youth. In the same way, when you are old and wrinkled, you'll be able to look at your child and see yourself in your prime. But if you choose not to have a child to remember you, you'll die alone and leave no memory of your own image.

4

Unthrifty loveliness, why dost thou spend
Upon thyself thy beauty's legacy?
Nature's bequest gives nothing, but doth lend,
And, being frank, she lends to those are free.
Then, beauteous niggard, why dost thou abuse
The bounteous largess given thee to give?
Profitless usurer, why dost thou use
So great a sum of sums yet canst not live?
For having traffic with thyself alone,
Thou of thyself thy sweet self dost deceive.
Then how when nature calls thee to be gone,
What acceptable audit canst thou leave?
   Thy unused beauty must be tombed with thee,
   Which usèd lives th' executor to be.

4

You wasteful lovely person, why are you spending all of your beauty on yourself? Nature doesn't give us anything; she only lends us the gifts we get at birth, and, being generous herself, she lends the most to people who are generous themselves. So, you beautiful miser, why do you abuse the bountiful gifts that were given to you to share with others? Why do you insist on being such a bad investor, using up the immense treasure you have to offer the world but unable to support yourself or preserve your memory? By only having dealings with yourself, you're cheating yourself out of the best part of yourself. Then how, when nature says it's time for you to go, will you be able to give an acceptable account of how you spent your time and beauty? Your unused beauty will have to be buried with you. But if you used that beauty now, it would stay behind once you were gone and preserve your legacy.

5

Those hours that with gentle work did frame
The lovely gaze where every eye doth dwell
Will play the tyrants to the very same
And that unfair which fairly doth excel.
For never-resting time leads summer on
To hideous winter and confounds him there,
Sap checked with frost and lusty leaves quite gone,
Beauty o'er-snowed and bareness everywhere.
Then were not summer's distillation left,
A liquid prisoner pent in walls of glass,
Beauty's effect with beauty were bereft,
Nor it nor no remembrance what it was.
    But flowers distilled, though they with winter meet,
    Leese but their show; their substance still lives sweet.

5

The same process that over time shaped your wonderful face, so that now everybody loves to look at you, will eventually destroy that face, making ugly what is now surpassingly beautiful. For never-resting Time takes summer by the hand, leads him into horrifying winter, and destroys him there—freezing his sap, removing his full leaves, covering up his beauty with snow, and turning everything bare. If we didn't have perfume distilled from summer flowers to keep in a jar, the effects of summer would vanish at the end of the season. Without perfume, we'd have no way of remembering the summer itself or its beauty. But the flowers used to make perfume lose only their outward beauty when winter comes; their beautiful scent lives on sweetly.

6

Then let not winter's ragged hand deface
In thee thy summer, ere thou be distilled.
Make sweet some vial; treasure thou some place
With beauty's treasure, ere it be self-killed.
That use is not forbidden usury
Which happies those that pay the willing loan;
That's for thyself to breed another thee,
Or ten times happier, be it ten for one.
Ten times thyself were happier than thou art,
If ten of thine ten times refigured thee.
Then what could death do if thou shouldst depart,
Leaving thee living in posterity?
   Be not self-willed, for thou art much too fair
   To be death's conquest and make worms thine heir.

6

(Continuing from Sonnet 5) So don't let wintry old age destroy your summer beauty before your essence has been preserved. Make some woman pregnant and pass on your beauty before it dies with you. It's unfair to charge exorbitant interest on a loan. But if you lend a woman your body, she'll be only too happy to pay you back with a child. Having a child—making another version of yourself—will make you happy. Having ten children will make you ten times as happy. What power would death have over you if you left children behind to keep your legacy alive? Don't be willful and selfish—you're much too beautiful to be conquered by death, with nothing left of you but a corpse devoured by worms.

7

Lo, in the Orient when the gracious light
Lifts up his burning head, each under eye
Doth homage to his new-appearing sight,
Serving with looks his sacred majesty;
And having climbed the steep-up heavenly hill,
Resembling strong youth in his middle age,
Yet mortal looks adore his beauty still,
Attending on his golden pilgrimage.
But when from highmost pitch, with weary car,
Like feeble age he reeleth from the day,
The eyes, 'fore duteous, now converted are
From his low tract and look another way.
  So thou, thyself out-going in thy noon,
  Unlooked on diest unless thou get a son.

7

When the gracious light of the sun rises in the east, each person on earth pays homage to it by gazing upon all its sacred majesty. And even at noon, once the sun has climbed the steep path to the top of the sky, it still looks like a strong young man in his prime and human beings still adore its beauty, watching it pass on its way like a golden king making a pilgrimage. But when the sun grows weary and falls from its highest point, it reels like an old man, and the people who once looked up at it so dutifully stop looking and turn the other way. In the same way, you, wasting your sexual energy in the prime of your life, will die alone and unloved unless you father a son.

8

Music to hear, why hear'st thou music sadly?
Sweets with sweets war not, joy delights in joy.
Why lov'st thou that which thou receiv'st not gladly,
Or else receiv'st with pleasure thine annoy?
If the true concord of well-tuned sounds,
By unions married, do offend thine ear,
They do but sweetly chide thee, who confounds
In singleness the parts that thou shouldst bear.
Mark how one string, sweet husband to another,
Strikes each in each by mutual ordering,
Resembling sire and child and happy mother,
Who all in one, one pleasing note do sing;
    Whose speechless song, being many, seeming one,
    Sings this to thee: "Thou single wilt prove none."

8

You're like music to listen to, so why does listening to music make you sad? Delightful and joyful things should complement one another. So why do you love things that make you unhappy and enjoy things that are bad for you? If music played well and in tune sounds bad to you, it's because that music is rebuking you for not playing your own part—not making your own harmony—by getting married and having children. Notice how the sound of two strings vibrating together in harmony is like a father and child and happy mother, who all sing one pleasing note together. Though their music has no words, the unity of their voices sings this warning to you: If you stay single, you'll be a childless nobody.

9

Is it for fear to wet a widow's eye
That thou consum'st thyself in single life?
Ah, if thou issueless shalt hap to die,
The world will wail thee like a makeless wife;
The world will be thy widow and still weep,
That thou no form of thee hast left behind,
When every private widow well may keep,
By children's eyes, her husband's shape in mind.
Look what an unthrift in the world doth spend
Shifts but his place, for still the world enjoys it;
But beauty's waste hath in the world an end,
And kept unused, the user so destroys it.
    No love toward others in that bosom sits
    That on himself such murd'rous shame commits.

9

Are you eating up your own life by remaining single because you're afraid your widow will cry when you die? Ah, if you happen to die childless, the entire world will mourn for you like a wife who's lost her husband. The world will be your widow and weep forever about the fact that you didn't leave a copy of yourself. But if you had left a wife behind, she'd have had her children to look at and remind her of her husband. A person who wastes his money is just shifting money around—at least the money's still in the world. But if beauty is wasted, the world loses it forever: If a beautiful person doesn't use his beauty, he destroys it. The person who would commit such a murderous outrage on himself has no love in his heart for others.

10

For shame deny that thou bear'st love to any,
Who for thyself art so unprovident.
Grant if thou wilt, thou art belov'd of many,
But that thou none lov'st is most evident;
For thou art so possessed with murd'rous hate
That 'gainst thyself thou stick'st not to conspire,
Seeking that beauteous roof to ruinate
Which to repair should be thy chief desire.
O change thy thought, that I may change my mind.
Shall hate be fairer lodged than gentle love?
Be as thy presence is, gracious and kind,
Or to thyself at least kind-hearted prove.
   Make thee another self for love of me,
   That beauty still may live in thine or thee.

10

If you have any sense of shame, admit that you don't have any love in your heart for anyone, since you're so unwilling to care about yourself. I'll admit, if you like, that many people love you, but it's also obvious that you love no one. For you are so possessed with murderous hatred that you have no problem plotting against yourself, seeking to destroy the house that you should want to repair. Oh, change your way of thinking, so I can change my mind about you. Should hate have a more beautiful home than love? Be gracious and kind, like your appearance—or at least be kindhearted to yourself. Have a child out of love for me, so your beauty will live on in your children, if not in you.

11

As fast as thou shalt wane, so fast thou grow'st
In one of thine, from that which thou departest;
And that fresh blood which youngly thou bestow'st
Thou mayst call thine when thou from youth convertest.
Herein lives wisdom, beauty, and increase;
Without this, folly, age, and cold decay.
If all were minded so, the times should cease,
And threescore year would make the world away.
Let those whom nature hath not made for store,
Harsh, featureless, and rude, barrenly perish.
Look whom she best endowed, she gave the more,
Which bounteous gift thou shouldst in bounty cherish.
  She carved thee for her seal, and meant thereby
  Thou shouldst print more, not let that copy die.

11

As fast as you will decline, you could grow again just as fast, through one of your children. The youth and vigor that you would pass on to a child now that you're still young, you could call your own when you're no longer young. In marriage and childbirth lie wisdom, beauty, and reproduction. Without them you have only foolishness, age, and the cold decay of death. If everyone thought like you, the human race would end, and in sixty years there'd be no more world. Let the people who aren't good enough to preserve—the rough, ugly, poor people—die childless. Nature gave abundantly to the people whom she endowed with beauty, and you should cherish her gifts by being generous with them. Nature made you her stamp, to serve as a template for all human beauty. She meant for you to make copies of yourself, so that the original—you—wouldn't die.

12

When I do count the clock that tells the time,
And see the brave day sunk in hideous night;
When I behold the violet past prime,
And sable curls all silvered o'er with white;
When lofty trees I see barren of leaves,
Which erst from heat did canopy the herd,
And summer's green all girded up in sheaves
Borne on the bier with white and bristly beard;
Then of thy beauty do I question make,
That thou among the wastes of time must go,
Since sweets and beauties do themselves forsake
And die as fast as they see others grow,
   And nothing 'gainst Time's scythe can make defense
   Save breed to brave him when he takes thee hence.

NO FEAR SHAKESPEARE

12

When I look at the clock and notice time ticking away, and see splendid day sink into hideous night; when I see the violet wilt and curly black hair turn white with age; when I see tall trees that once provided shade for herds now barren of leaves, and the summer's crops tied up and hauled to the barn as if summer itself were an old man being carried off to his grave—then I have doubts about the fate of your beauty, since you too will have to undergo the ravages of time. Sweet and beautiful creatures don't stay that way; they die as fast as they see others grow. And there's no defense against Time's destructive power, except perhaps to have children—to defy Time when he takes you away.

13

O that you were yourself! But, love, you are
No longer yours than you yourself here live.
Against this coming end you should prepare,
And your sweet semblance to some other give.
So should that beauty which you hold in lease
Find no determination; then you were
Yourself again after yourself's decease,
When your sweet issue your sweet form should bear.
Who lets so fair a house fall to decay,
Which husbandry in honor might uphold
Against the stormy gusts of winter's day
And barren rage of death's eternal cold?
   O, none but unthrifts, dear my love you know,
   You had a father; let your son say so.

NO FEAR SHAKESPEARE

13

Oh, how I wish you were yourself! But, my love, your identity will only last as long as you're alive. You should make preparations in anticipation of your inevitable death and pass on your beautiful appearance to someone else. That way, your beauty, which you've only borrowed, wouldn't have to end. Then, even after you died, your beautiful body would be renewed in your children. Who would let such a beautiful house fall into disrepair when prudent maintenance might make it outlast the stormy gusts of winter and the frustrating barrenness surrounding death? Only the most irresponsible spender could do such a thing, you know, my dear love. You had a father—let your son be able to say the same.

14

Not from the stars do I my judgment pluck,
And yet methinks I have astronomy,
But not to tell of good or evil luck,
Of plagues, of dearths, or seasons' quality;
Nor can I fortune to brief minutes tell,
Pointing to each his thunder, rain, and wind,
Or say with princes if it shall go well,
By oft predict that I in heaven find;
But from thine eyes my knowledge I derive,
And, constant stars, in them I read such art
As truth and beauty shall together thrive,
If from thyself to store thou wouldst convert;
    Or else of thee this I prognosticate:
    Thy end is truth's and beauty's doom and date.

14

I don't base my judgments on the stars, and yet it does seem to me I know astrology. I can't foresee good or bad events—predict plagues, famines, or what a season will be like. Nor can I predict down to the minute what each person's misfortunes are going to be. Nor can I tell princes whether things will go well for them by looking at the heavens. But I can forecast the future by looking in your eyes. I see by those reliable guides that truth and beauty will thrive if you would only pass your attributes on to a child. Otherwise, this is what I predict: When you die, truth and beauty will die with you.

15

When I consider every thing that grows
Holds in perfection but a little moment;
That this huge stage presenteth nought but shows
Whereon the stars in secret influence commént;
When I perceive that men as plants increase,
Cheerèd and checked ev'n by the self-same sky,
Vaunt in their youthful sap, at height decrease,
And wear their brave state out of memory;
Then the conceit of this inconstant stay
Sets you, most rich in youth, before my sight,
Where wasteful time debateth with decay,
To change your day of youth to sullied night;
   And all in war with time for love of you,
   As he takes from you, I engraft you new.

15

When I think about the fact that every living thing is perfect only for a brief time, that the whole world is one big stage on which the stars secretly control the action; when I see that men grow like plants, encouraged and then thwarted by the same sky, exulting in their youthful vigor and then declining just when they're at their height, vanishing until their glory is no longer even remembered; when I think about the whole world's instability—then I think of you, a youth enjoying so many of nature's rich gifts. In my mind, I see time and decay debating with each other about how to corrupt your sunny youth, how to convert it to old age and night. Out of love for you, I wage war against time: As he takes away your youth, I continually recreate you in these poems.

16

But wherefore do not you a mightier way
Make war upon this bloody tyrant, time,
And fortify yourself in your decay
With means more blessèd than my barren rhyme?
Now stand you on the top of happy hours,
And many maiden gardens, yet unset,
With virtuous wish would bear your living flowers,
Much liker than your painted counterfeit.
So should the lines of life that life repair
Which this time's pencil or my pupil pen
Neither in inward worth nor outward fair
Can make you live yourself in eyes of men.
   To give away yourself keeps yourself still,
   And you must live, drawn by your own sweet skill.

16

(Continuing from Sonnet 15) But why not take advantage of a stronger way to fight against this bloody tyrant, Time, and strengthen yourself in your old age in a happier way than with my useless sonnets? Now your capacity for pleasure is at its peak, and many virtuous maidens would love to marry you and bear your children, who would recreate your image much better than any artificial reproduction such as a painting or poem. The faces of your children will renew your life. Time created you and brought you to your present state of perfection, but it cannot preserve your inner worth or outer beauty, and neither can my poetry. Having a baby would preserve your image and ensure that you live on by your own design.

17

Who will believe my verse in time to come
If it were filled with your most high deserts?
Though yet heav'n knows it is but as a tomb
Which hides your life and shows not half your parts.
If I could write the beauty of your eyes
And in fresh numbers number all your graces,
The age to come would say, "This poet lies—
Such heavenly touches ne'er touched earthly faces."
So should my papers, yellowed with their age,
Be scorned, like old men of less truth than tongue,
And your true rights be termed a poet's rage
And stretchèd meter of an ántique song;
　　But were some child of yours alive that time,
　　You should live twice: in it and in my rhyme.

17

Who in the future will ever believe my poetry if I praise you as you deserve? Though, I have to admit, my poetry is like a tomb that actually hides what you are really like and doesn't manage to show even half of your true qualities. If I could capture in my writing how beautiful your eyes are and create new verses to list all of your wonderful attributes, decades from now people would say, "This poet lies. No human face was ever so divine." In this way, my poems (yellowed with age), would be scorned, like old men who talk too much without saying anything true, and what is really your due would be dismissed as a poet's madness, the false verses of an old song. But if some child of yours were still alive then, you would live twice: in the child, and in my poetry.

18

Shall I compare thee to a summer's day?
Thou art more lovely and more temperate.
Rough winds do shake the darling buds of May,
And summer's lease hath all too short a date.
Sometime too hot the eye of heaven shines,
And often is his gold complexion dimmed;
And every fair from fair sometime declines,
By chance or nature's changing course untrimmed.
But thy eternal summer shall not fade,
Nor lose possession of that fair thou ow'st,
Nor shall death brag thou wand'rest in his shade,
When in eternal lines to time thou grow'st.
   So long as men can breathe or eyes can see,
   So long lives this, and this gives life to thee.

18

Shall I compare you to a summer day? You're lovelier
and milder. Rough winds shake the pretty buds of
May, and summer doesn't last nearly long enough.
Sometimes the sun shines too hot, and often its golden
face is darkened by clouds. And everything beautiful
stops being beautiful, either by accident or simply in
the course of nature. But your eternal summer will
never fade, nor will you lose possession of your
beauty, nor shall death brag that you are wandering in
the underworld, once you're captured in my eternal
verses. As long as men are alive and have eyes with
which to see, this poem will live and keep you alive.

19

Devouring Time, blunt thou the lion's paws,
And make the earth devour her own sweet brood;
Pluck the keen teeth from the fierce tiger's jaws,
And burn the long-lived phoenix in her blood;
Make glad and sorry seasons as thou fleet'st,
And do whate'er thou wilt, swift-footed time,
To the wide world and all her fading sweets;
But I forbid thee one most heinous crime:
O carve not with thy hours my love's fair brow,
Nor draw no lines there with thine ántique pen.
Him in thy course untainted do allow
For beauty's pattern to succeeding men.
   Yet do thy worst, old Time; despite thy wrong,
   My love shall in my verse ever live young.

19

Devouring Time, go ahead and blunt the lion's paws.
Make the earth swallow up her own creatures. Pluck
the sharp teeth out of the fierce tiger's jaws, and burn
the long-lived phoenix in its own blood. Make happy
and sad times as you fly by, and do whatever you want,
swift-footed Time, to the wide world and all its vanishing delights. But I forbid you to commit one heinous crime. Oh, don't carve wrinkles into my love's
beautiful forehead, and don't draw lines there with
your old pen. Let him pass through time untainted, to
serve as the model of beauty for men to come. But do
your worst, old Time. Despite your wrongs, my love
will stay young forever in my poetry.

20

A woman's face, with nature's own hand painted,
Hast thou, the master-mistress of my passion;
A woman's gentle heart, but not acquainted
With shifting change, as is false women's fashion;
An eye more bright than theirs, less false in rolling,
Gilding the object whereupon it gazeth;
A man in hue, all hues in his controlling,
Which steals men's eyes and women's souls amazeth.
And for a woman wert thou first created,
Till nature as she wrought thee fell a-doting,
And by addition me of thee defeated,
By adding one thing to my purpose nothing.
　　But since she pricked thee out for women's pleasure,
　　Mine be thy love, and thy love's use their treasure.

20

Your face is as pretty as a woman's, but you don't even have to use makeup—you, the man (or should I say *woman?*) I love. Your heart is as gentle as a woman's, but it isn't cheating like theirs. Your eyes are prettier than women's, but not as roving—you bless everything you look at. You've got the good looks of a handsome man, but you attract both women *and* men. When Mother Nature made you, she originally intended to make you a woman, but then she got carried away with her creation and screwed me by adding a certain *thing* that I have no use for. But since she gave you a prick to please women, I'll keep your love, and they can enjoy your body.

21

So is it not with me as with that muse,
Stirred by a painted beauty to his verse,
Who heav'n itself for ornament doth use,
And every fair with his fair doth rehearse—
Making a couplement of proud compare
With sun and moon, with earth and sea's rich gems,
With April's first-born flow'rs, and all things rare
That heaven's air in this huge rondure hems.
O let me, true in love but truly write,
And then believe me: my love is as fair
As any mother's child, though not so bright
As those gold candles fixed in heaven's air.
    Let them say more that like of hearsay well;
    I will not praise that purpose not to sell.

NO FEAR SHAKESPEARE

21

I'm not like that other poet who writes about a woman who's pretty because she wears a lot of makeup. In his verses, he compares her to heaven itself, and to every other beautiful thing—the sun and moon, the rich gems of earth and sea, the first flowers of April, and all the rest of the precious things on the face of the earth. Since I really *am* in love, I just want to write the truth, and when I do, believe me—my lover is as beautiful as any human being, though maybe not as bright as the stars. Whoever actually likes those love-poem clichés can say more; I'm not trying to sell anything, so I won't waste time with praise.

22

My glass shall not persuade me I am old
So long as youth and thou are of one date;
But when in thee time's furrows I behold,
Then look I death my days should expiate.
For all that beauty that doth cover thee
Is but the seemly raiment of my heart,
Which in thy breast doth live, as thine in me.
How can I then be elder than thou art?
O therefore, love, be of thyself so wary
As I, not for myself, but for thee will,
Bearing thy heart, which I will keep so chary
As tender nurse her babe from faring ill.
   Presume not on thy heart when mine is slain;
   Thou gav'st me thine not to give back again.

22

I won't believe my mirror when it tells me I'm old, as long as you're still young. But when I see you with wrinkles, then I'll know death is on its way, because your beauty is as close to my heart as beautiful clothing to a body. Put another way, my heart beats in your chest and yours in mine. But if that's true, then how can I be older than you? Therefore, my love, take care of yourself just as I will take care of myself, not for my own sake, but because I have your heart inside of me, which I will protect as carefully as a nurse her baby. Don't expect to get your heart back from me when mine is dead. You gave it to me forever, never to be returned.

23

As an unperfect actor on the stage,
Who with his fear is put besides his part,
Or some fierce thing replete with too much rage,
Whose strength's abundance weakens his own heart;
So I, for fear of trust, forget to say
The perfect ceremony of love's rite,
And in mine own love's strength seem to decay,
O'ercharged with burden of mine own love's might.
O let my books be then the eloquence
And dumb presagers of my speaking breast,
Who plead for love and look for recompense
More than that tongue that more hath more expressed.
    O learn to read what silent love hath writ!
    To hear with eyes belongs to love's fine wit.

23

Like an actor who hasn't learned his lines perfectly and forgets his part because of stage fright, or like some raging animal or human whose excessive passion makes it weak, so I, because I can't trust myself, forget to say the things a lover should say to his darling; just when my love is strongest it seems to be getting weak. So let my writings speak for my heart instead. They plead for love better than I could if I spoke, even if I said more and more eloquently. Oh, read in these silent lines the love I cannot express in speech. Love will give you the insight to read between the lines.

24

Mine eye hath played the painter and hath steeled
Thy beauty's form in table of my heart.
My body is the frame wherein 'tis held,
And pérspective it is best painter's art.
For through the painter must you see his skill
To find where your true image pictured lies,
Which in my bosom's shop is hanging still,
That hath his windows glazèd with thine eyes.
Now see what good turns eyes for eyes have done:
Mine eyes have drawn thy shape, and thine for me
Are windows to my breast, wherethrough the sun
Delights to peep, to gaze therein on thee.
    Yet eyes this cunning want to grace their art;
    They draw but what they see, know not the heart.

24

My eye has acted like a painter and engraved your beautiful image on the canvas of my heart. My body is the frame that holds this picture; to draw that picture with perspective, realistically representing depth, is the highest skill a painter could have. Only via this painter—my eye—can you find the image of you that dwells continually in my heart: Your own eyes are the windows into my heart. Now look at the favors our eyes have done for each other: My eyes have drawn your shape, and your eyes are windows into which I can look to see my own heart, into which the sun also likes to look, taking a peep at your reflection. Yet my eyes lack a certain skill that would grace the others they already have: They can only draw what they see; they don't see into your heart.

25

Let those who are in favor with their stars
Of public honor and proud titles boast,
Whilst I, whom fortune of such triumph bars,
Unlooked for joy in that I honor most.
Great princes' favorites their fair leaves spread
But as the marigold at the sun's eye,
And in themselves their pride lies burièd,
For at a frown they in their glory die.
The painful warrior famousèd for worth,
After a thousand victories once foiled,
Is from the book of honor razèd quite,
And all the rest forgot for which he toiled.
   Then happy I that love and am belovèd
   Where I may not remove nor be removèd.

25

Let fortunate people boast about their prizes and their titles, while I—who am not lucky enough to get such rewards—experience unexpected joy in what I honor most: your love. Those courtiers who enjoy high status because they're the favorites of great princes are like marigolds. They bloom as long as the sun shines on them, but their pride is fragile—one frown will kill them. And once a famous warrior who has painfully endured and won a thousand battles is defeated, he's stripped of all his honors, and all of the successes that he worked for are forgotten. How much happier am I, who love and am loved in a place I cannot leave and from which others cannot remove me.

26

Lord of my love, to whom in vassalage
Thy merit hath my duty strongly knit,
To thee I send this written embassage,
To witness duty, not to show my wit.
Duty so great, which wit so poor as mine
May make seem bare, in wanting words to show it,
But that I hope some good conceit of thine
In thy soul's thought, all naked, will bestow it.
Till whatsoever star that guides my moving
Points on me graciously with fair aspéct
And puts apparel on my tattered loving,
To show me worthy of thy sweet respect.
    Then may I dare to boast how I do love thee;
    Till then, not show my head where thou mayst prove me.

NO FEAR SHAKESPEARE

26

My love, I am your absolute servant; your worth compels me to serve you loyally. I'm sending you this message to show my devotion to you, not to show that I can write well. My skills are so poor that I may make my obligation to you, which is great, seem meager. I don't have the words to express it properly. But I hope that in your heart you'll form an idea of what I mean and the idea will enrich your sense of what I owe you. When the star that guides me shines on me favorably, giving me the inspiration to dress up my tattered love for you in clever words that prove I'm worthy of your sweet respect—that's when I'll dare to boast about how much I love you. Until then, I won't show my face anywhere that you can put me to the test.

27

Weary with toil, I haste me to my bed,
The dear repose for limbs with travail tired;
But then begins a journey in my head
To work my mind, when body's work's expired.
For then my thoughts, from far where I abide,
Intend a zealous pilgrimage to thee,
And keep my drooping eyelids open wide,
Looking on darkness which the blind do see.
Save that my soul's imaginary sight
Presents thy shadow to my sightless view,
Which, like a jewel hung in ghastly night,
Makes black night beauteous, and her old face new.
   Lo thus by day my limbs, by night my mind,
   For thee, and for myself, no quiet find.

27

Weary from work, I hasten to my bed, the sweet place of rest for a body tired out from laboring. But then I start to go on a journey in my head, making my mind work after my body's work is finished. Because when I go to bed, my thoughts begin the trip from where I am, far away from you, to where you are. They keep my weary eyes wide open, staring at the darkness like blind people do. Except, in my imagination, I see your image, though it's too dark to see anything else. Like a shining jewel hanging in the terrifying night, your image makes that old, black night look beautiful and young. See, because of you, my body does not rest in the daytime and my mind finds no peace at night.

28

How can I then return in happy plight
That am debarred the benefit of rest?
When day's oppression is not eased by night,
But day by night and night by day oppressed?
And each, though enemies to either's reign,
Do in consent shake hands to torture me,
The one by toil, the other to complain
How far I toil, still farther off from thee.
I tell the day to please him thou art bright,
And dost him grace when clouds do blot the heaven.
So flatter I the swart-complexioned night,
When sparkling stars twire not, thou gild'st the even.
   But day doth daily draw my sorrows longer,
   And night doth nightly make grief's length seem stronger.

28

(Continuing from Sonnet 27) So how can I return in a cheerful state of mind when I'm prevented from getting any rest? When the oppression I experience during the day isn't relieved by any sleep at night, but instead my sleepless nights oppress me during the day and my wearisome days oppress me at night? And though day and night are natural enemies, they've shook hands and made a bargain to both torture me, the day with labor, the night with thoughts of how far away you are as I labor over thoughts of you. I try to please the day by telling him how bright you are—so bright that you take the sun's place when clouds cover the sky. In the same way, I use you to flatter black night, telling him how you brighten the evening sky when stars don't shine. But they both—day and night—only prolong my sorrows, and night by night this prolonged grief grows stronger.

29

When in disgrace with fortune and men's eyes
I all alone beweep my outcast state,
And trouble deaf heav'n with my bootless cries,
And look upon myself, and curse my fate,
Wishing me like to one more rich in hope,
Featured like him, like him with friends possessed,
Desiring this man's art, and that man's scope,
With what I most enjoy contented least;
Yet in these thoughts myself almost despising,
Haply I think on thee, and then my state,
Like to the lark at break of day arising
From sullen earth, sings hymns at heaven's gate.
   For thy sweet love remembered such wealth brings
   That then I scorn to change my state with kings.

29

When I'm in disgrace with everyone and my luck has deserted me, I sit all alone and cry about the fact that I'm an outcast, and bother God with useless cries, which fall on deaf ears, and look at myself and curse my fate, wishing that I had more to hope for, wishing I had this man's good looks and that man's friends, this man's skills and that man's opportunities, and totally dissatisfied with the things I usually enjoy the most. Yet, as I'm thinking these thoughts and almost hating myself, I happen to think about you, and then my condition improves—like a lark at daybreak rising up and leaving the earth far behind to sing hymns to God. For when I remember your sweet love, I feel so wealthy that I'd refuse to change places even with kings.

30

When to the sessions of sweet silent thought
I summon up remembrance of things past,
I sigh the lack of many a thing I sought,
And with old woes new wail my dear time's waste.
Then can I drown an eye unused to flow,
For precious friends hid in death's dateless night,
And weep afresh love's long since cancelled woe,
And moan th' expense of many a vanished sight.
Then can I grieve at grievances foregone,
And heavily from woe to woe tell o'er
The sad account of fore-bemoanèd moan,
Which I new pay as if not paid before.
   But if the while I think on thee, dear friend,
   All losses are restored, and sorrows end.

30

When I sit alone in silence and remember the past, I get depressed about all the things I don't have that I once strived for, and I add to old griefs new tears for all the valuable time I've wasted. Then I can drown my eyes, which are not usually wet from crying, in tears for precious friends who are dead, and I can weep again for hurts in loves that are long since over and moan about the loss of many things I'll never see again. Then I can grieve about grievances I had let go of and sadly recount each woe that I'd already cried about in the past, feeling the pain all over again, as if I hadn't suffered over these things already. But if I think about you, my dear friend, while I'm doing all of this, I get back everything I'd lost, and all my sorrows end.

31

Thy bosom is endearèd with all hearts
Which I, by lacking, have supposèd dead;
And there reigns love, and all love's loving parts,
And all those friends which I thought burièd.
How many a holy and obsequious tear
Hath dear religious love stol'n from mine eye
As interest of the dead, which now appear
But things removed that hidden in thee lie.
Thou art the grave where buried love doth live,
Hung with the trophies of my lovers gone,
Who all their parts of me to thee did give;
That due of many now is thine alone.
    Their images I loved I view in thee,
    And thou, all they, hast all the all of me.

NO FEAR SHAKESPEARE

31

You have the love of everyone who used to love me, people who I supposed were dead because I didn't have their love anymore. Love reigns in your heart—both everything belonging to love and all those friends who I thought were dead and buried. How many tears of devoted love have I shed at funerals, in payment to the dead, when now it appears they had only gone to hide in your heart. You're like a grave where dead lovers come alive again, decorated with mementos of those lost loves who gave you all the love I owed to each of them. All the love I owed to many is now yours alone. I see these lovers in you, and you, who contain everyone I have ever loved or was loved by, have all of me.

32

If thou survive my well-contented day,
When that churl death my bones with dust shall cover,
And shalt by fortune once more re-survey
These poor rude lines of thy deceasèd lover,
Compare them with the bett'ring of the time,
And though they be outstripped by every pen,
Reserve them for my love, not for their rhyme,
Exceeded by the height of happier men.
O then vouchsafe me but this loving thought:
"Had my friend's muse grown with this growing age,
A dearer birth than this his love had brought
To march in ranks of better equipage.
    But since he died and poets better prove,
    Theirs for their style I'll read, his for his love."

32

If you survive me, living on after dust covers my bones, and you should happen to read over again these poor, crude sonnets written by the man who once loved you, remember that things have improved since my day. So even though any poet today could write better sonnets, keep my poems for the sake of my love, not for my skill, which luckier men have far surpassed. And grant me this loving thought: "If my friend's inspiration was paired with the advantages today's poets have, his love would have brought forth better poems than these, to rank alongside those of today's better poets. But since he died, and poets are better now, I'll read their poems for their style, his for his love."

33

Full many a glorious morning have I seen
Flatter the mountain tops with sovereign eye,
Kissing with golden face the meadows green,
Gilding pale streams with heavenly alchemy,
Anon permit the basest clouds to ride
With ugly rack on his celestial face,
And from the fórlorn world his visage hide,
Stealing unseen to west with this disgrace.
Ev'n so my sun one early morn did shine
With all triumphant splendor on my brow;
But out alack, he was but one hour mine;
The region cloud hath masked him from me now.
   Yet him for this my love no whit disdaineth.
   Suns of the world may stain when heav'n's sun staineth.

NO FEAR SHAKESPEARE

33

I've seen many beautiful mornings in which the sun beautifies the mountaintops, kissing the green meadows with its golden face and making streams sparkle as if by magic. But then it suddenly permits the nastiest clouds to ride across its heavenly face, and it hides from the forlorn world, sneaking off to the west in disgrace. In exactly this way, early one morning *my* sun shone on my face with triumphant splendor, but alas he was only mine for one hour. The clouds have hidden him from me now. But I don't fault him for this at all. Golden men like him can disgrace themselves as much as the real sun does.

In Sonnets 33–34, the speaker uses the image of the sun being covered by clouds as a metaphor for his being betrayed by the young man he loves.

34

Why didst thou promise such a beauteous day
And make me travel forth without my cloak,
To let base clouds o'ertake me in my way,
Hiding thy brav'ry in their rotten smoke?
'Tis not enough that through the cloud thou break,
To dry the rain on my storm-beaten face.
For no man well of such a salve can speak
That heals the wound and cures not the disgrace.
Nor can thy shame give physic to my grief;
Though thou repent, yet I have still the loss.
The offender's sorrow lends but weak relief
To him that bears the strong offense's cross.
   Ah, but those tears are pearl which thy love sheds,
   And they are rich, and ransom all ill deeds.

34

Sun, why did you make it look like today was going to be such a beautiful day, so that I went out without my cloak, only to let nasty clouds overtake me on my way, hiding your radiance behind their poisonous mist? It's not enough that you broke through the clouds and dried the rain off my storm-beaten face, because no man can be satisfied with a cure that heals the physical injury but doesn't take away the disgrace. Nor does it comfort me that you're ashamed, because even though you regret what you did, I have still lost out. When someone takes something away from you, their being sorry doesn't help much. Ah, but those tears you're shedding out of love for me are like pearls— very valuable ones—and they make up for all your bad deeds.

35

No more be grieved at that which thou hast done.
Roses have thorns, and silver fountains mud;
Clouds and eclipses stain both moon and sun,
And loathsome canker lives in sweetest bud.
All men make faults, and even I in this,
Authórizing thy trespass with compare,
Myself corrupting, salving thy amiss,
Excusing these sins more than these sins are.
For to thy sensual fault I bring in sense—
Thy adverse party is thy advocate—
And 'gainst myself a lawful plea commence.
Such civil war is in my love and hate
    That I an áccessory needs must be
    To that sweet thief which sourly robs from me.

35

Don't be upset anymore about what you did. Everything has its bad side: Roses have thorns, sparkling fountains have mud, the sun and the moon are periodically covered up by clouds and eclipses, and disgusting worms live in the sweetest flowers. All men do bad things—even me, right now: As I excuse your transgression by comparing it to other things, I corrupt myself by making excuses for your misdeeds (more excuses for these little sins than they even require). Because what I'm doing is taking your sins, which were just physical urges, and putting my mind to work on their behalf. The person you've hurt is now advocating for you—I'm now pleading the case against myself. I'm so conflicted between love and hate that I can't resist helping that sweet villain who bitterly injures me every hour.

36

Let me confess that we two must be twain,
Although our undivided loves are one.
So shall those blots that do with me remain
Without thy help by me be borne alone.
In our two loves there is but one respect,
Though in our lives a separable spite,
Which, though it alter not love's sole effect,
Yet doth it steal sweet hours from love's delight.
I may not evermore acknowledge thee,
Lest my bewailèd guilt should do thee shame;
Nor thou with public kindness honor me,
Unless thou take that honor from thy name.
   But do not so; I love thee in such sort,
   As, thou being mine, mine is thy good report.

36

I acknowledge that the two of us have to part, even though we're united in love. That way I can take those disgraces that we've incurred together all onto myself, bearing them without any help from you. Our love for one another gives us common cause, despite this awful situation that forces us apart, which, though it can't prevent us from being united in love, still robs us of sweet hours of pleasure together. I can never greet you openly again, because my guilt would bring shame upon you. Nor can you ever honor me with public kindness without dishonoring your own reputation. But don't do that. I love you so much that I value your good reputation as my own.

37

As a decrepit father takes delight
To see his active child do deeds of youth,
So I, made lame by fortune's dearest spite,
Take all my comfort of thy worth and truth.
For whether beauty, birth, or wealth, or wit,
Or any of these all, or all, or more,
Entitled in thy parts do crownèd sit,
I make my love engrafted to this store.
So then I am not lame, poor, nor despised,
Whilst that this shadow doth such substance give
That I in thy abundance am sufficed,
And by a part of all thy glory live.
    Look what is best, that best I wish in thee.
    This wish I have; then ten times happy me.

37

Just as a decrepit father takes pleasure in seeing his active child engaging in youthful activities, so I, whom misfortune has injured and crippled, take all the comfort I can in your good worth and fidelity. For whether beauty, nobility, wealth, and intelligence—or any one of these, or all of them, or more than these—are your princely attributes, I'm attaching my love to them. I'm not lame, poor, or despised, as long as this fantasy of mine lets me take so much satisfaction in your good luck and I can live off part of your glory. Whatever is best, that's what I wish you to have. Since I have this wish, I'm lucky ten times over.

38

How can my muse want subject to invent
While thou dost breathe, that pour'st into my verse
Thine own sweet argument, too excellent
For every vulgar paper to rehearse?
O give thyself the thanks, if aught in me
Worthy perusal stand against thy sight.
For who's so dumb that cannot write to thee,
When thou thyself dost give invention light?
Be thou the tenth muse, ten times more in worth
Than those old nine which rhymers invocate;
And he that calls on thee, let him bring forth
Eternal numbers to outlive long date.
   If my slight muse do please these curious days,
    The pain be mine, but thine shall be the praise.

38

How could I lack things to write about while you're alive? You pour inspiration into my poetry by giving me the sweetest subject to write about: yourself—too excellent a subject for ordinary writers to describe. Oh, give yourself the credit if you see anything in my writing that's worth reading. For who is so speechless that he can't write to you, when you yourself provide the creative spark? You should be the tenth muse, worth ten times more than those other nine invoked by poets. And whoever calls on you for inspiration, let him write eternal verses, to outlive even the farthest reaches of time. If my little bit of inspiration happens to please today's demanding readers, the painful work can be mine, but the praise shall be yours.

39

O how thy worth with manners may I sing,
When thou art all the better part of me?
What can mine own praise to mine own self bring,
And what is't but mine own when I praise thee?
Even for this, let us divided live,
And our dear love lose name of single one,
That by this separation I may give
That due to thee which thou deserv'st alone.
O absence, what a torment wouldst thou prove,
Were it not thy sour leisure gave sweet leave
To entertain the time with thoughts of love,
Which time and thoughts so sweetly dost deceive,
　And that thou teachest how to make one twain,
　By praising him here who doth hence remain.

39

How can I celebrate your worth in my poems without appearing conceited, given that you're my better half? What good does it do me to praise myself—and am I doing anything besides praising myself when I praise you? For this reason, let's live apart. And though we love each other dearly, let's lose our common identity; by this separation, I can give you the praise that you deserve by yourself. Oh, absence, you would be such a torment if it weren't for the fact that you give me the chance to fill up the lonely hours with thoughts of love, which make the time pass so sweetly, and that you teach me how to divide my love and me in two, as I, here, praise my friend while he remains elsewhere.

40

Take all my loves, my love; yea, take them all.
What hast thou then more than thou hadst before?
No love, my love, that thou mayst true love call.
All mine was thine before thou hadst this more.
Then if for my love thou my love receivest,
I cannot blame thee, for my love thou usest.
But yet be blamed, if thou thyself deceivest
By wilful taste of what thyself refusest.
I do forgive thy robb'ry, gentle thief,
Although thou steal thee all my poverty;
And yet love knows it is a greater grief
To bear love's wrong than hate's known injury.
  Lascivious grace, in whom all ill well shows,
  Kill me with spites; yet we must not be foes.

40

Take all my loves, my love—yes, take them all: Take my love for you, take away your love for me, and take a lover from me. What do you have now that you didn't have before? My love, you haven't acquired true love, because my true love was yours to begin with, before you took this extra from me. If, instead of accepting my love, you make love to the person, love, I can't blame you, because you're only taking advantage of my love. But, you *should* be blamed if you deceive yourself by taking from one person what you won't take from another—if you willingly make love to one person while refusing to make love to me. I forgive you for stealing from me, gentle thief, although you're taking the little I have. And yet every lover knows that it hurts more to be injured by a lover than by an enemy. You, who are gracious even when succumbing to lust, you in whom everything bad looks good—even if you kill me with injuries, let's not become enemies.

41

Those pretty wrongs that liberty commits
When I am sometime absent from thy heart,
Thy beauty and thy years full well befits,
For still temptation follows where thou art.
Gentle thou art, and therefore to be won;
Beauteous thou art, therefore to be assailed;
And when a woman woos, what woman's son
Will sourly leave her till he have prevailed?
Ay me, but yet thou might'st my seat forbear,
And chide thy beauty and thy straying youth,
Who lead thee in their riot even there
Where thou art forced to break a twofold truth:
    Hers by thy beauty tempting her to thee,
    Thine by thy beauty being false to me.

41

Those charming little infidelities that you commit when I'm away from you for awhile are understandable given your youth and beauty, since you're continually tempted wherever you go. You're noble and distinguished, so women see you as a prize catch. You're beautiful, and therefore women pursue you aggressively. And when a woman is the pursuer, what man will rudely refuse her to get his point across? But, oh my—you might at least stay away from my mistress and keep your beauty and youthful urges in line, as they're leading you into debauchery, which breaks two bonds: my mistress's fidelity to me, which your beauty tempts her to break, and your bond with me, which your beauty, again, lets you break.

42

That thou hast her it is not all my grief,
And yet it may be said I loved her dearly;
That she hath thee is of my wailing chief,
A loss in love that touches me more nearly.
Loving offenders, thus I will excuse ye:
Thou dost love her because thou knowst I love her;
And for my sake even so doth she abuse me,
Suff'ring my friend for my sake to approve her.
If I lose thee, my loss is my love's gain,
And losing her, my friend hath found that loss;
Both find each other, and I lose both twain,
And both for my sake lay on me this cross.
   But here's the joy; my friend and I are one;
   Sweet flatt'ry! Then she loves but me alone.

NO FEAR SHAKESPEARE

42

The fact that you now have my mistress isn't the only reason I'm hurt, though it's true that I loved her dearly. What makes me cry the most is that now she has you, a loss of love that hurts me even more. You two criminals in love, here's how I'll rationalize the pain you've caused me: You, friend, love her because you know I love her. And she loves you for the exact same reason, putting up with your praises and love-making for my sake, because she knows you're my friend. If I lose you, it's a win for my mistress. And if I lose her, you will have found what I've lost. Both of the people I love find each other, and I lose them both, and both cause me this pain. But here's what makes me happy: My friend and I are one person. How gratifying!—It turns out my mistress loves only me.

43

When most I wink, then do mine eyes best see,
For all the day they view things unrespected;
But when I sleep, in dreams they look on thee,
And, darkly bright, are bright in dark directed.
Then thou, whose shadow shadows doth make bright—
How would thy shadow's form form happy show
To the clear day with thy much clearer light,
When to unseeing eyes thy shade shines so?
How would, I say, mine eyes be blessèd made
By looking on thee in the living day,
When in dead night thy fair imperfect shade
Through heavy sleep on sightless eyes doth stay?
    All days are nights to see till I see thee,
    And nights bright days when dreams do show thee me.

NO FEAR SHAKESPEARE

43

My eyes work best when I'm asleep, because all day they look at things I don't care about. When I sleep, my dreaming eyes alight on you and glitter brightly in the dark, having found your bright image there. Given that your shadowy dream-image brightens even the dark, how bright might you appear in daylight, when your own light is so much clearer? How bright, when your shadow shines so brightly to my eyes blinded by darkness? What good would it do my eyes to see you in the daytime when they already look at your beautiful image in the dead of night, as I sleep? Every day is as dark as night until I get to see you again, and every night is as bright as day when I see you in my dreams.

44

If the dull substance of my flesh were thought,
Injurious distance should not stop my way;
For then, despite of space, I would be brought
From limits far remote where thou dost stay.
No matter then although my foot did stand
Upon the farthest earth removed from thee,
For nimble thought can jump both sea and land
As soon as think the place where he would be.
But ah, thought kills me that I am not thought
To leap large lengths of miles when thou art gone,
But that so much of earth and water wrought,
I must attend time's leisure with my moan,
    Receiving naughts by elements so slow
    But heavy tears, badges of either's woe.

44

If I were made of thought instead of slow, dull flesh, this wicked distance between us wouldn't keep me from where I wanted to be. No matter the distance— from the farthest possible regions—I would bring myself to where you are. It wouldn't matter that my feet were standing on the spot on earth farthest from you: Thought is nimble enough to jump over both sea and land as quickly as it can think about the place it wants to be. But, ah, it's killing me to think that I'm not made of thought and can't leap over the many miles when you are gone. Instead my body is made of so much earth and water that I have to fill the long time without you with my moans. The leaden, deep earth and slow, wet water of which I am made give me nothing but heavy tears.

The speaker alludes to the belief that all matter is made up of four elements: earth, water, air, and fire. Earth and water were believed to be the heaviest, most tangible elements.

45

The other two, slight air and purging fire,
Are both with thee, wherever I abide;
The first my thought, the other my desire,
These present absent with swift motion slide.
For when these quicker elements are gone
In tender embassy of love to thee,
My life, being made of four, with two alone
Sinks down to death, oppressed with melancholy;
Until life's composition be recured
By those swift messengers returned from thee,
Who ev'n but now come back again, assured
Of thy fair health, recounting it to me.
   This told, I joy, but then no longer glad,
   I send them back again and straight grow sad.

NO FEAR SHAKESPEARE

45

This sonnet, like Sonnet 44, is based on the idea that matter is composed of the four elements: earth, water, air, and fire.

The speaker refers to the Renaissance notion that melancholy, or depression, is caused by an imbalance of substances within the body.

The other two elements, weightless air and purifying fire, both remain with you, wherever I may be. Air is my thoughts, and fire is my desire. The two of them slide back and forth between us swiftly and effortlessly. Normally I am made up of all four elements, but when my air and fire are off on their errand of love to you, I sink into depression and slide toward death, until air and fire return to restore the proper balance within me. Even now, they have returned from you to tell me that you're well and in good health. I rejoice to hear this but then immediately grow gloomy from missing you, so I send them back to you and immediately grow sad again.

46

Mine eye and heart are at a mortal war
How to divide the conquest of thy sight;
Mine eye my heart thy picture's sight would bar;
My heart mine eye the freedom of that right.
My heart doth plead that thou in him dost lie,
A closet never pierced with crystal eyes;
But the defendant doth that plea deny,
And says in him thy fair appearance lies.
To 'cide this title is empanellèd
A quest of thoughts, all tenants to the heart,
And by their verdict is determinèd
The clear eye's moiety and the dear heart's part:
  As thus—mine eye's due is thy outward part,
  And my heart's right, thy inward love of heart.

46

My eye and my heart have gone to war with each other. They're fighting over who gets to control your image. My eye wants to bar my heart from the image that it formed, while my heart wants to keep my eye away from *its* image. My heart insists that your image lies safely hidden inside of him, protected from eyes, which give everything away. But my eye, the defendant, denies the charges and argues that your beauty resides in him. To decide whose claim is right, I have assembled a jury consisting of my thoughts, all of which owe allegiance to the heart. And they have delivered a verdict to determine which portion of your image belongs to the eyes and which precious portion to the heart. This is what they say: My eyes have the rights to your outward appearance, and my heart has the right to love you and be loved by you.

47

Betwixt mine eye and heart a league is took,
And each doth good turns now unto the other.
When that mine eye is famished for a look,
Or heart in love with sighs himself doth smother,
With my love's picture then my eye doth feast
And to the painted banquet bids my heart.
Another time mine eye is my heart's guest,
And in his thoughts of love doth share a part.
So either by thy picture or my love,
Thyself away are present still with me;
For thou no farther than my thoughts canst move,
And I am still with them, and they with thee;
   Or if they sleep, thy picture in my sight
   Awakes my heart to heart's and eye's delight.

47

My eye and my heart have reached an agreement, and now each does the other favors. When my eye is starving to take a look at you or my heart smothers itself with sighs of love for you, then my eye feasts on a painting of you and invites my heart to join in the banquet and stare at the painting too. On another occasion, my eye is the guest with whom my heart shares some of his thoughts of love. So when you are gone, you're still present with me, either through your painting or in my love for you: You can't travel farther than my thoughts, and I'm always with them, and they are always with you. Even if my thoughts go to sleep, your painting will wake up my heart and delight both heart and eyes.

48

How careful was I, when I took my way,
Each trifle under truest bars to thrust,
That to my use it might unusèd stay
From hands of falsehood, in sure wards of trust.
But thou, to whom my jewels trifles are,
Most worthy comfort, now my greatest grief,
Thou best of dearest, and mine only care,
Art left the prey of every vulgar thief.
Thee have I not locked up in any chest,
Save where thou art not, though I feel thou art,
Within the gentle closure of my breast,
From whence at pleasure thou mayst come and part;
   And even thence thou wilt be stol'n, I fear,
   For truth proves thievish for a prize so dear.

NO FEAR SHAKESPEARE

48

I used to be so careful when I'd travel to secure all my trivial possessions with the most reliable locks available so criminals wouldn't tamper with them. But you, so much more precious than my jewels and my greatest comfort, have become my greatest sadness and worry, because you're vulnerable to any common thief. I haven't locked you up in any chest, other than in my own chest, where my heart is, and you're not really there, even though I feel that you are. You can come and go from my heart as you please, and I'm afraid you'll be stolen from there, because even an honest man would turn thief to get such a rich prize.

49

Against that time (if ever that time come)
When I shall see thee frown on my defects;
Whenas thy love hath cast his utmost sum,
Called to that audit by advised respects;
Against that time when thou shalt strangely pass,
And scarcely greet me with that sun, thine eye;
When love, converted from the thing it was,
Shall reasons find of settled gravity;
Against that time do I ensconce me here
Within the knowledge of mine own desert,
And this my hand against myself uprear
To guard the lawful reasons on thy part:
   To leave poor me, thou hast the strength of laws,
   Since why to love I can allege no cause.

49

In anticipation of the time, if it ever comes, when I will see you frown at my defects; when mature reflection tells you that you've come to the end of your love for me; in anticipation of that time when you will pass by me like a stranger, barely even acknowledging me with a glance of your brilliant eye; when your love for me isn't love anymore and you're guided only by somber judgment—in anticipation of that time, I'm establishing myself here, knowing how little I really deserve, and I'm giving testimony against myself to defend the justice of your future actions. You have every right to leave poor me—all the laws of reason back you up—since I can't offer any justification for your loving me.

50

How heavy do I journey on the way
When what I seek (my weary travel's end)
Doth teach that ease and that repose to say,
"Thus far the miles are measured from thy friend."
The beast that bears me, tired with my woe,
Plods dully on to bear that weight in me,
As if by some instinct the wretch did know
His rider loved not speed, being made from thee.
The bloody spur cannot provoke him on
That sometimes anger thrusts into his hide,
Which heavily he answers with a groan,
More sharp to me than spurring to his side;
    For that same groan doth put this in my mind:
    My grief lies onward and my joy behind.

50

I feel very depressed as I go on my journey, because I know when I get where I'm going I'll have time and leisure to rest, and when I have that time to rest I'll have nothing to think about except "I'm this many miles away from my friend." The horse that carries me, affected by my sadness, plods slowly on, bearing the weight of my emotions, as if by some instinct the poor creature knew that I didn't want to move quickly away from you. I can't provoke him to go any faster with the bloody spur that I sometimes thrust into his hide in anger. He only answers me with a groan, which hurts me more than my spur hurts him, because it reminds me that my grief lies ahead of me and all my joy is behind me.

51

Thus can my love excuse the slow offense
Of my dull bearer, when from thee I speed:
From where thou art, why should I haste me thence?
Till I return, of posting is no need.
O what excuse will my poor beast then find,
When swift extremity can seem but slow?
Then should I spur, though mounted on the wind;
In wingèd speed no motion shall I know:
Then can no horse with my desire keep pace;
Therefore desire, of perfect'st love being made,
Shall neigh no dull flesh in his fiery race,
But love, for love, thus shall excuse my jade:
  Since from thee going he went wilful slow,
  Towards thee I'll run, and give him leave to go.

51

(Continuing from Sonnet 50) This is how my love for you excuses my horse's slow plod as I journey away from you: "Why *should* I hurry away from you?" Until I return, there's no need to rush. But what excuse will my poor horse have for his slowness then, when even the most extreme swiftness will seem slow to me? On the return journey I'd use my spurs even if the animal rode like the wind. Even if my horse had wings I'd feel like we were standing still. No horse could keep up with my desire then. My desire, made of the most perfect love, will race toward you like a horse made of fire, not neigh like a slow, dull horse made of flesh and blood. But, my love, out of love I'll excuse my horse like this: Since he deliberately went slowly as he was leaving you, I'll run back to you and forget about the horse altogether.

52

So am I as the rich whose blessèd key
Can bring him to his sweet up-lockèd treasure,
The which he will not every hour survey,
For blunting the fine point of seldom pleasure.
Therefore are feasts so solemn and so rare,
Since seldom coming in the long year set,
Like stones of worth they thinly placèd are,
Or captain jewels in the carcanet.
So is the time that keeps you as my chest,
Or as the wardrobe which the robe doth hide,
To make some special instant special blest
By new unfolding his imprisoned pride.
  Blessèd are you whose worthiness gives scope,
  Being had, to triumph; being lacked, to hope.

52

I'm like a rich man who has the key to a great treasure chest, but who resists opening it every hour, because he doesn't want to spoil his pleasure by getting too used to the treasure. That's why holiday feasts are so infrequent: Spaced out across the year, they're like precious jewels placed evenly across a crown. In the same way, the time that keeps us apart is *my* treasure chest, or it's like a closet that hides a beautiful robe—the closet makes a special occasion even more special when it is opened to reveal its hidden splendor. You are blessed with such great worth that those who are with you feel triumphant, and those who are not with you hope to be.

53

What is your substance, whereof are you made,
That millions of strange shadows on you tend?
Since everyone hath every one, one shade,
And you, but one, can every shadow lend.
Describe Adonis, and the counterfeit
Is poorly imitated after you.
On Helen's cheek all art of beauty set,
And you in Grecian tires are painted new.
Speak of the spring and foison of the year;
The one doth shadow of your beauty show,
The other as your bounty doth appear,
And you in every blessèd shape we know.
   In all external grace you have some part,
   But you like none, none you, for constant heart.

53

Adonis: a mytho-
logical youth who
was so beautiful
that Venus,
the goddess of
love, fell in love
with him

Helen: a famously
beautiful woman
over whom the
Trojan War
was begun

What is your true essence, what are you made of, that there should be millions of reflections of you? Every person has only one image, but you, though you're only one person, lend something to everyone else's image. If an artist tries to depict Adonis, he'll wind up creating an inferior imitation of you. If he were to paint Helen as beautifully as possible, he would again wind up with a picture of you, decked out in Greek costume. Praise the spring and the abundant harvest season—but the spring is only a faint shadow of your beauty, and the fall a faint imitation of your abundance. We recognize you in every blessed sight that we see. You are part of every beautiful thing, but you're not like any of them—you're incomparable—in the constancy of your heart.

54

O how much more doth beauty beauteous seem
By that sweet ornament which truth doth give!
The rose looks fair, but fairer we it deem
For that sweet odor which doth in it live.
The canker-blooms have full as deep a dye
As the perfumèd tincture of the roses,
Hang on such thorns, and play as wantonly,
When summer's breath their maskèd buds discloses;
But for their virtue only is their show,
They live unwooed, and unrespected fade,
Die to themselves. Sweet roses do not so;
Of their sweet deaths are sweetest odors made;
   And so of you, beauteous and lovely youth;
   When that shall vade, my verse distills your truth.

54

Beauty seems so much more beautiful when it comes with honesty and integrity. Roses are beautiful, but we think they're even more so because of their sweet scent. Wildflowers have as deep a color as fragrant roses; their thorns are the same, and their beauty broadcasts just as loudly when summer opens their buds. But because their only virtue is their looks, no one wants or respects them and they die unnoticed and alone. Sweet roses don't suffer that fate. When they die, the most fragrant perfumes are made from their corpses. The same is true of you, beautiful youth. When you fade away, my poems will preserve your essence.

55

Not marble nor the gilded monuments
Of princes shall outlive this pow'rful rhyme,
But you shall shine more bright in these conténts
Than unswept stone, besmeared with sluttish time.
When wasteful war shall statues overturn,
And broils root out the work of masonry,
Nor Mars his sword, nor war's quick fire, shall burn
The living record of your memory.
'Gainst death and all oblivious enmity
Shall you pace forth; your praise shall still find room
Even in the eyes of all posterity
That wear this world out to the ending doom.
  So till the judgment that yourself arise,
   You live in this, and dwell in lovers' eyes.

NO FEAR SHAKESPEARE

55

Neither marble nor the gold-plated monuments of princes will outlive this powerful poetry. You will shine more brightly in these poems than those stones that crumble to dust, blackened by time. When devastating war overturns statues, with its battles uprooting buildings, neither the god of war nor his quick-burning fires shall destroy this record of you. Despite death and ignorant enmity, you shall continue on. All those generations to come, down to the weary end of time, will devote space to praising you. So until Judgment Day, when you are raised up, you will live in this poetry, and in the eyes of lovers who read this.

56

Sweet love, renew thy force; be it not said
Thy edge should blunter be than appetite,
Which but today by feeding is allayed,
Tomorrow sharpened in his former might.
So love be thou; although today thou fill
Thy hungry eyes even till they wink with fullness,
Tomorrow see again, and do not kill
The spirit of love with a perpetual dullness.
Let this sad int'rim like the ocean be
Which parts the shore, where two contracted new
Come daily to the banks, that when they see
Return of love, more blest may be the view;
   Else call it winter, which being full of care,
   Makes summer's welcome, thrice more wished, more rare.

NO FEAR SHAKESPEARE

56

The speaker is addressing love the emotion, not an individual.

Sweet love, be as strong as you used to be. Don't let people say that love is less keen and persistent than lust, which may be satiated today but then comes back tomorrow just as strong and sharp as ever. That's how you should be, love. Although today you see so much of your love that you want to shut your eyes, look again tomorrow: Do not kill your affection by making yourself perpetually dull and lethargic. Let this sad period of separation be like an ocean that lies between two opposite shores; two newly betrothed lovers come every day to the opposite banks hoping to see each other, and when they do, the sight feels especially blessed. Or call this time winter, which, being full of misery, makes us wish for summer three times more than if it didn't feel so rare.

57

Being your slave, what should I do but tend
Upon the hours and times of your desire?
I have no precious time at all to spend,
Nor services to do, till you require.
Nor dare I chide the world without end hour
Whilst I, my sovereign, watch the clock for you,
Nor think the bitterness of absence sour
When you have bid your servant once adieu.
Nor dare I question with my jealous thought
Where you may be, or your affairs suppose,
But, like a sad slave, stay and think of nought
Save, where you are, how happy you make those.
   So true a fool is love that in your will,
   Though you do anything, he thinks no ill.

57

Since I'm your slave, what else should I do but wait on the hours, and for the times when you'll want me? I don't have any valuable time to spend, or any services to do, until you need me. Nor do I dare complain about how agonizingly long the hours are while I watch the clock for you, my king, or how bitter your absence is after you've said goodbye to your servant. Nor do I dare ask jealous questions about where you might be, or speculate about your affairs, but like a sad slave I sit still and think about nothing except how happy you're making whomever you're with. Love makes a person such a faithful fool that no matter what you do to satisfy your desires, he doesn't think you've done anything wrong.

58

That god forbid, that made me first your slave,
I should in thought control your times of pleasure,
Or at your hand th' account of hours to crave,
Being your vassal bound to stay your leisure.
O let me suffer, being at your beck,
Th' imprisoned absence of your liberty;
And patience tame to sufferance bide each check,
Without accusing you of injury.
Be where you list, your charter is so strong
That you yourself may privilege your time
To what you will; to you it doth belong
Yourself to pardon of self-doing crime.
    I am to wait, though waiting so be hell,
    Not blame your pleasure, be it ill or well.

NO FEAR SHAKESPEARE

58

(Continuing from Sonnet 57) Whatever god decided to make me your slave, may he never allow me to so much as think about having any control over when you see me, or asking you to account for how you've been passing the hours. I'm your slave, after all, and forced to wait until you have time for me. Oh, while I wait for your summons, let me suffer patiently the prison of this lengthy absence from you as you do whatever you want. And let me control my impatience and quietly endure each disappointment without accusing you of hurting me. Go wherever you want—you're so privileged that you may decide to do whatever you like. You have the right to pardon yourself for any crime you commit. And I have to wait, even if it feels like hell, and not blame you for following your desire, whether it's for good or bad.

59

If there be nothing new, but that which is
Hath been before, how are our brains beguiled,
Which, lab'ring for invention, bear amiss
The second burthen of a former child!
O that recórd could with a backward look,
Ev'n of five hundred courses of the sun,
Show me your image in some ántique book,
Since mind at first in character was done,
That I might see what the old world could say
To this composèd wonder of your frame;
Whether we are mended, or where better they,
Or whether revolution be the same.
    O sure I am the wits of former days
    To subjects worse have giv'n admiring praise.

59

If it's true that there's nothing new and everything that now exists existed in the past, then we are really fooling ourselves when we struggle to write something new, winding up, after much exhausting, painful labor, with a tired imitation of an imitation! If only I could look back into the records, even as far as five hundred years ago, and find a description of you in some old book, written when people were just beginning to put their thoughts in writing, so I could see what the old world would say about your amazingly beautiful body. Then I could see whether we've gotten better at writing or worse, or whether things have stayed the same as the world revolves. Oh, I'm sure the witty writers of the past have devoted praise and admiration to worse subjects than you.

60

Like as the waves make towards the pebbled shore,
So do our minutes hasten to their end,
Each changing place with that which goes before,
In sequent toil all forwards do contend.
Nativity, once in the main of light,
Crawls to maturity, wherewith being crowned,
Crooked eclipses 'gainst his glory fight,
And time that gave doth now his gift confound.
Time doth transfix the flourish set on youth
And delves the parallels in beauty's brow;
Feeds on the rarities of nature's truth,
And nothing stands but for his scythe to mow.
　　And yet to times in hope my verse shall stand,
　　Praising thy worth, despite his cruel hand.

60

As the waves move toward the pebbled shore, so do the minutes we have to live hasten toward their end, each moment changing place with the one before, striving to move forward with successive efforts. Everything that has been born, though it once swam in that broad ocean of light that exists before birth, crawls its way up the shores of maturity, where it faces cruel obstacles to its glory. Time, which gives everything, now destroys its own gift. Time pierces the beauty of youth, drawing wrinkles in beauty's forehead. Time devours the choicest specimens of nature; nothing exists that it won't mow down with its scythe. And yet my verses will last into the future, praising your worth despite Time's cruel hand.

61

Is it thy will thy image should keep open
My heavy eyelids to the weary night?
Dost thou desire my slumbers should be broken,
While shadows like to thee do mock my sight?
Is it thy spirit that thou send'st from thee
So far from home into my deeds to pry,
To find out shames and idle hours in me,
The scope and tenor of thy jealousy?
O no; thy love, though much, is not so great.
It is my love that keeps mine eye awake,
Mine own true love that doth my rest defeat,
To play the watchman ever for thy sake.
   For thee watch I whilst thou dost wake elsewhére,
   From me far off, with others all too near.

61

Was it your intention that I should stay awake all night thinking about you? Do you want my sleep to be interrupted while I'm tantalized by mental images of you? Are you sending your spirit far from its home to pry into my dealings, to find out the shameful things I've been up to in idle hours? Are you jealous? Oh, no: Though you love me a great deal, you don't love me that much. It's *my* love for *you* that's keeping me awake. My own true love keeps me from sleeping—staying up worrying about you. I stay up for you, while you are awake somewhere else: far away from me, but all too close to certain other people.

62

Sin of self-love possesseth all mine eye
And all my soul, and all my every part;
And for this sin there is no remedy,
It is so grounded inward in my heart.
Methinks no face so gracious is as mine,
No shape so true, no truth of such account;
And for myself mine own worth do define,
As I all other in all worths surmount.
But when my glass shows me myself indeed,
Beated and chopped with tanned antiquity,
Mine own self-love quite contrary I read;
Self so self-loving were iniquity.
   'Tis thee, myself, that for myself I praise,
   Painting my age with beauty of thy days.

62

The sin of self-love controls everything I see, and my entire soul, and every part of me. There's no way to get rid of this sin, it's so deeply rooted in my heart. I think that no one's face is as gracious as mine, no body so evenly proportioned, no one's integrity of such high worth. I calculate my value such that I surpass everybody else in everything. But when my mirror shows me how I really look, beaten and cracked by age and the sun, I come to an opposite conclusion: For myself to love myself so much would be a sinful error. It's you I'm praising when I praise myself, ornamenting my old age with the beauty of your youth.

63

Against my love shall be as I am now,
With time's injurious hand crushed and o'erworn;
When hours have drained his blood and filled his brow
With lines and wrinkles; when his youthful morn
Hath traveled on to age's steepy night,
And all those beauties whereof now he's king
Are vanishing or vanished out of sight,
Stealing away the treasure of his spring;
For such a time do I now fortify
Against confounding age's cruel knife,
That he shall never cut from memory
My sweet love's beauty, though my lover's life.
  His beauty shall in these black lines be seen,
  And they shall live, and he in them still green.

NO FEAR SHAKESPEARE

63

In anticipation of the time when my love shall be as I am now, crushed and worn out by time's damaging hand; when time has sapped his vigor and filled his forehead with wrinkles; when his youthful morning has moved on to the difficult night of old age, and all of those forms of beauty that he now possesses are disappearing, or already gone, robbing him of the treasures of his youth—in anticipation of that time, I'm now defending myself against the cruel knife of time, ensuring that he never cuts from my memory the beauty of my sweet love, even if he takes my lover's life. My lover's beauty will remain visible in these black lines of poetry, and these lines shall survive, and he will live on in them, still young.

64

When I have seen by time's fell hand defaced
The rich proud cost of outworn buried age;
When sometime lofty towers I see down-razed,
And brass eternal slave to mortal rage;
When I have seen the hungry ocean gain
Advantage on the kingdom of the shore,
And the firm soil win of the watery main,
Increasing store with loss, and loss with store;
When I have seen such interchange of state,
Or state itself confounded to decay,
Ruin hath taught me thus to ruminate,
That time will come and take my love away.
   This thought is as a death, which cannot choose
   But weep to have that which it fears to lose.

64

Now that I have seen time's terrible hand deface the costly and splendid monuments of buried men from ages past, and once-lofty towers torn down; now that I have seen even hard brass subject to perpetual destruction by human beings; now that I have seen the hungry ocean swallow up the land and firm land seize territory from the ocean, so that each one's loss is the other's gain; now that I have seen that all things constantly change into something else or fall into decay—all this destruction has taught me to think: The time will come in which time will take my love from me. This thought feels like death, and makes me weep over what I have that I'm afraid of losing.

65

Since brass, nor stone, nor earth, nor boundless sea,
But sad mortality o'ersways their power,
How with this rage shall beauty hold a plea,
Whose action is no stronger than a flower?
O how shall summer's honey breath hold out
Against the wrackful siege of batt'ring days,
When rocks impregnable are not so stout,
Nor gates of steel so strong but time decays?
O fearful meditation! Where, alack,
Shall time's best jewel from time's chest lie hid?
Or what strong hand can hold his swift foot back?
Or who his spoil or beauty can forbid?
   O none, unless this miracle have might,
   That in black ink my love may still shine bright.

65

Since neither brass nor stone nor earth nor the limit-less ocean is strong enough to resist the sad force of mortality, how can beauty possibly resist death's rage when beauty is no stronger than a flower? How could your beauty, which is as fragile as the sweet breath of summer, hold out against the destructive assaults of time when neither invulnerable rocks nor gates of steel are strong enough to resist its decaying power? What a frightening thing to think about! Alas, where can I put your beauty, time's most precious creation, to hide it from time itself? Whose hand is strong enough to slow time down? Who will forbid its destruction of your beauty? Oh, no one, unless this miracle proves effective: that in the black ink of my poetry, the one I love may still shine bright.

66

Tired with all these, for restful death I cry,
As to behold desert a beggar born,
And needy nothing trimmed in jollity,
And purest faith unhappily forsworn,
And gilded honor shamefully misplaced,
And maiden virtue rudely strumpeted,
And right perfection wrongfully disgraced,
And strength by limping sway disablèd,
And art made tongue-tied by authority,
And folly, doctor-like, controlling skill,
And simple truth miscalled simplicity,
And captive good attending captain ill.
   Tired with all these, from these would I be gone,
   Save that to die, I leave my love alone.

66

Because I'm tired of all of these things, I cry out for restful death: deserving people destined to be beggars, and worthless people dressed up in fancy clothes, and sacred vows broken, and rewards and honors shamefully bestowed on the wrong people, and chaste women turned into whores, and people perfectly in the right disgraced with slander, and the strong disabled by authorities who are weak, and artists silenced by authority, and fools controlling the wise like a doctor does the sick, and simple truth mistaken for simplemindedness, and good enslaved by evil. I'm tired of all these things and would like to escape them, except that if I die I'll be leaving the person I love all alone.

67

Ah, wherefore with infection should he live,
And with his presence grace impiety,
That sin by him advantage should achieve
And lace itself with his society?
Why should false painting imitate his cheek,
And steal dead seeing of his living hue?
Why should poor beauty indirectly seek
Roses of shadow, since his rose is true?
Why should he live, now nature bankrupt is,
Beggared of blood to blush through lively veins?
For she hath no exchequer now but his,
And, proud of many, lives upon his gains.
  O him she stores, to show what wealth she had
  In days long since, before these last so bad.

NO FEAR SHAKESPEARE

67

(Continuing from Sonnet 66) Ah, why should the man I love have to live in the midst of all this corruption, gracing sinners with his presence so they can take advantage of their association with him? Why should portrait painters and makeup artists be allowed to imitate his face, making lifeless copies of his vibrant beauty? Why should those less beautiful than he imitate roses by false means, when he is a true rose? And why should he live, now that Nature has degenerated so much that she can hardly infuse anyone with vigor and beauty? Because she has no fund of beauty now except him and, having so many children to provide for, needs to borrow from his store. Oh, Nature keeps him alive in order to show the wealth of beauty she had long ago, before these recent bad days came.

68

Thus is his cheek the map of days outworn,
When beauty lived and died as flow'rs do now,
Before these bastard signs of fair were born,
Or durst inhabit on a living brow;
Before the golden tresses of the dead,
The right of sepulchers, were shorn away,
To live a second life on second head;
Ere beauty's dead fleece made another gay.
In him those holy ántique hours are seen,
Without all ornament, itself and true,
Making no summer of another's green,
Robbing no old to dress his beauty new;
    And him as for a map doth nature store,
    To show false art what beauty was of yore.

68

(Continuing from Sonnet 67) So his face is the incarnation of how things were in the old days, when beautiful people lived and died as commonly as flowers—before these illegitimate signs of beauty were created, or anyone dared to put them on a living human being. That was before the golden locks of corpses, which belong in graves, were cut off and made to live a second life on a second person's head. It was before the hair of a beautiful corpse served to make another person happy. You can see the old-fashioned youthful beauty of his face: no wig to ornament it, the real thing in all its honesty, not borrowing someone else's youth nor stealing from the old to look new again. Nature preserves him as a map, to show cosmetics what beauty used to be.

69

Those parts of thee that the world's eye doth view
Want nothing that the thought of hearts can mend.
All tongues, the voice of souls, give thee that due,
Utt'ring bare truth, ev'n so as foes commend.
Thy outward thus with outward praise is crowned;
But those same tongues that give thee so thine own
In other accents do this praise confound
By seeing farther than the eye hath shown.
They look into the beauty of thy mind,
And that in guess they measure by thy deeds;
Then, churls, their thoughts (although their eyes were kind)
To thy fair flower add the rank smell of weeds;
    But why thy odor matcheth not thy show,
    The soil is this, that thou dost common grow.

69

Those parts of you that are visible to the world lack nothing, and no one could imagine improving them. Everybody admits this unreservedly, though they're only saying what's obviously true—what even your enemies praise you for. Thus, your outside is rewarded with public praise. But the same people who give you the praise your beauty deserves take quite another tack once they've looked beyond the surface. These people examine the beauty of your mind and character, and they guess at what's in there by observing your actions. Then, though they judged your appearance kindly, their harsh thoughts tell them that although you appear beautiful you smell corrupt. So, if you don't smell as good as you look, this is the reason: You're hanging out with lowlifes.

70

That thou art blamed shall not be thy defect,
For slander's mark was ever yet the fair;
The ornament of beauty is suspéct,
A crow that flies in heaven's sweetest air.
So thou be good, slander doth but approve
Thy worth the greater, being wooed of time;
For canker vice the sweetest buds doth love,
And thou present'st a pure unstainèd prime.
Thou hast passed by the ambush of young days,
Either not assailed, or victor being charged;
Yet this thy praise cannot be so thy praise,
To tie up envy evermore enlarged.
    If some suspéct of ill masked not thy show,
    Then thou alone kingdoms of hearts shouldst owe.

70

The fact that people say bad things about you won't be held against you, because beautiful people have always been the target of slander. Beautiful people are always the objects of suspicion, a black crow darkening heaven. As long as you're good, you're a target of temptation; slander just proves how worthy you are. For vice, like a worm, loves to devour the sweetest buds the most, which makes you—in your prime, pure and unstained—a perfect target. You've escaped the traps that usually endanger young men, because either no one tempted you or you resisted the temptation. However, this praise I've given you won't inflate your reputation so much that it keeps envious people from talking, because they always will. If your beauty weren't masked by at least some suspicion of evil, you'd be the most beloved person in the world.

71

No longer mourn for me when I am dead
Than you shall hear the surly sullen bell
Give warning to the world that I am fled
From this vile world with vildest worms to dwell:
Nay, if you read this line, remember not
The hand that writ it, for I love you so
That I in your sweet thoughts would be forgot,
If thinking on me then should make you woe.
O if, I say, you look upon this verse
When I perhaps compounded am with clay,
Do not so much as my poor name rehearse,
But let your love even with my life decay,
  Lest the wise world should look into your moan
  And mock you with me after I am gone.

71

When I am dead, mourn for me only as long as you hear the funeral bell telling the world that I've left this vile world to go live with the vile worms. No, if you read this line, don't remember who wrote it, because I love you so much that I'd rather you forgot me than thought about me and became sad. I'm telling you, if you look at this poem when I'm, say, dissolved in the earth, don't so much as utter my name but let your love die with me. Otherwise, the world, in all its wisdom, will investigate why you're sad and use me to mock you, now that I am gone.

72

O lest the world should task you to recite
What merit lived in me that you should love
After my death, dear love, forget me quite,
For you in me can nothing worthy prove;
Unless you would devise some virtuous lie,
To do more for me than mine own desert,
And hang more praise upon deceasèd I
Than niggard truth would willingly impart.
O lest your true love may seem false in this,
That you for love speak well of me untrue,
My name be buried where my body is,
And live no more to shame nor me nor you.
   For I am shamed by that which I bring forth,
   And so should you, to love things nothing worth.

72

(Continuing from Sonnet 71) Oh, in case the world challenges you to recite what merit I possessed that would justify your loving me, forget about me entirely after I die, dear love. For you won't find anything worthy to say about me unless you make up some generous lie, which makes me sound better than I deserve, and attach more praise to my dead self than accords with the stingy truth. Oh, to prevent your true love from becoming false, as it will, in part, if you make false statements out of love for me, let my name be buried with my corpse and no longer bring shame to you or me. For I'm ashamed of what I produce, and you should be, too, to love such worthless things.

73

That time of year thou mayst in me behold
When yellow leaves, or none, or few, do hang
Upon those boughs which shake against the cold,
Bare ruined choirs, where late the sweet birds sang.
In me thou seest the twilight of such day
As after sunset fadeth in the west,
Which by and by black night doth take away,
Death's second self, that seals up all in rest.
In me thou seest the glowing of such fire
That on the ashes of his youth doth lie,
As the deathbed whereon it must expire
Consumed with that which it was nourished by.
   This thou perceiv'st, which makes thy love more strong,
   To love that well which thou must leave ere long.

73

When you look at me, you can see an image of those times of year when the leaves are yellow or have fallen, or when the trees have no leaves at all and the bare branches where the sweet birds recently sang shiver in anticipation of the cold. In me you can see the twilight that remains after the sunset fades in the west, which by and by is replaced by black night, the twin of death, which closes up everyone in eternal rest. In me you can see the remains of a fire still glowing atop the ashes of its early stages, as if it lay on its own deathbed, on which it has to burn out, consuming what used to fuel it. You see all these things, and they make your love stronger, because you love even more what you know you'll lose before long.

74

But be contented when that fell arrest
Without all bail shall carry me away;
My life hath in this line some interest,
Which for memorial still with thee shall stay.
When thou reviewest this, thou dost review
The very part was consecrate to thee.
The earth can have but earth, which is his due;
My spirit is thine, the better part of me.
So then thou hast but lost the dregs of life,
The prey of worms, my body being dead,
The coward conquest of a wretch's knife,
Too base of thee to be rememb'red.
  The worth of that is that which it contains,
  And that is this, and this with thee remains.

NO FEAR SHAKESPEARE

74

(Continuing from Sonnet 73) But don't be upset when death arrives to carry me off where no one can release me. My life will continue to some extent in these lines, which you'll always have to remember me by. When you reread this, you'll be seeing again the precise part of me that was dedicated to you. The earth can only have the earthly part of me, which is what belongs to it. My spirit, the better part of me, is yours. So when I'm dead you'll have only my body—the dregs of my life, the part that worms eat, the only part of me that cowardly, wretched death could kill, the part that's too worthless for you to remember. What gives my body its worth is the spirit it contains, and that spirit is this poem, and this poem will remain with you.

75

So are you to my thoughts as food to life,
Or as sweet seasoned show'rs are to the ground;
And for the peace of you I hold such strife
As 'twixt a miser and his wealth is found;
Now proud as an enjoyer, and anon
Doubting the filching age will steal his treasure;
Now counting best to be with you alone,
Then bettered that the world may see my pleasure;
Sometime all full with feasting on your sight
And by and by clean starvèd for a look;
Possessing or pursuing no delight,
Save what is had or must from you be took.
   Thus do I pine and surfeit day by day,
   Or gluttoning on all, or all away.

75

I need you the way living things need food or the grass needs rain, and to attain the peace that only you can give me, I fight with myself the way a miser struggles with his wealth. One moment he enjoys his wealth proudly, and the next he's worried that someone from these thieving times will steal his treasure. One moment I think it's best to be alone with you, but then I think it would be better if the rest of the world could see my pleasure. At times I feel oversatisfied from looking at you excessively, but a little later I'm starving to get a look at you. I can't experience or pursue any enjoyment except what you can give me or I can take from you. That's why I suffer and feel hungry day after day, because I either get too much of you or none at all.

76

Why is my verse so barren of new pride,
So far from variation or quick change?
Why with the time do I not glance aside
To new-found methods and to compounds strange?
Why write I still all one, ever the same,
And keep invention in a noted weed,
That every word doth almost tell my name,
Showing their birth, and where they did proceed?
O know, sweet love, I always write of you,
And you and love are still my argument.
So all my best is dressing old words new,
Spending again what is already spent:
    For as the sun is daily new and old,
    So is my love still telling what is told.

76

Why is my poetry so lacking in new ornaments, so determined in avoiding variation and change? Why don't I, like everyone else these days, take a look at the new literary styles and weird combinations of other writers? Why do I always write the same thing, always the same, and always in the same distinctive style, so that almost every word I write tells you who wrote it, where it was born, and where it comes from? Oh, you should know, sweet love, I always write about you, and you and love are continually my subjects. So the best I can do is find new words to say the same thing, spending again what I've already spent: Just as the sun is new and old every day, my love for you keeps making me tell what I've already told.

77

Thy glass will show thee how thy beauties wear,
Thy dial how thy precious minutes waste;
The vacant leaves thy mind's imprínt will bear,
And of this book this learning mayst thou taste:
The wrinkles which thy glass will truly show
Of mouthèd graves will give thee memory;
Thou by thy dial's shady stealth mayst know
Time's thievish progress to eternity.
Look what thy memory cannot contain,
Commit to these waste blanks, and thou shalt find
Those children nursed, delivered from thy brain,
To take a new acquaintance of thy mind.
   These offices, so oft as thou wilt look,
   Shall profit thee and much enrich thy book.

77

Your mirror will show you how your beauty is wearing away; your clock how your precious minutes are slipping away; the pages of this blank notebook will record your thoughts; and you may learn the following things from those thoughts: The wrinkles that your mirror will show you will remind you of open graves. By the hands of your clock, you'll learn how time keeps stealing away to eternity. Write down whatever you can't remember on these blank pages, and later, when you encounter those thoughts again, the children of your brain, they'll have grown up, nourished by your continued reflection. They'll be like a new acquaintance. Doing these things often—looking in the mirror and at the clock, and writing in the book—will benefit you and greatly enrich your book.

78

So oft have I invoked thee for my muse,
And found such fair assistance in my verse,
As every alien pen hath got my use,
And under thee their poesy disperse.
Thine eyes, that taught the dumb on high to sing,
And heavy ignorance aloft to fly,
Have added feathers to the learnèd's wing
And given grace a double majesty.
Yet be most proud of that which I compile,
Whose influence is thine and born of thee.
In others' works thou dost but mend the style,
And arts with thy sweet graces gracèd be;
    But thou art all my art, and dost advance
    As high as learning my rude ignorance.

78

I have cited you as my source of inspiration so often, and you've helped my poetry so much, that every other writer has adopted my habit of addressing poems to you, and now they all write their poetry in your name. Your beautiful eyes are such a source of inspiration that they've helped the mute sing high notes, raised the ignorant to new heights of intelligence, helped the educated soar even higher, and enhanced the gracefulness of the graceful. Yet your greatest pride should be in my accomplishment, because it's done under your influence and inspired by you. With other writers, you only improve their style, adding an extra sheen to the skill they already have. But without you I have no skill at all; you lift up my utter ignorance so that I am well-educated.

79

Whilst I alone did call upon thy aid,
My verse alone had all thy gentle grace,
But now my gracious numbers are decayed,
And my sick muse doth give another place.
I grant, sweet love, thy lovely argument
Deserves the travail of a worthier pen,
Yet what of thee thy poet doth invent
He robs thee of and pays it thee again.
He lends thee virtue, and he stole that word
From thy behavior; beauty doth he give
And found it in thy cheek; he can afford
No praise to thee but what in thee doth live.
   Then thank him not for that which he doth say,
   Since what he owes thee thou thyself dost pay.

79

When I was the only writer who looked to you for inspiration, only my poetry received all of the benefits of your noble grace. But now the poems I write under your inspiration have gotten worse, and I'm forced to make room for someone else. I admit, my sweet love, that such a lovely subject as you deserves to have a better writer working for you. But whatever your new poet says about you, he's only stealing the ideas from you and giving them back to you. He says you're virtuous, but he only learned that word from watching your behavior. He says you're beautiful, but he only found out about beauty from your face. He has no praise to give you except for what he finds in you already. So don't thank him for what he says about you, since you're paying for everything he gives you.

80

O how I faint when I of you do write,
Knowing a better spirit doth use your name,
And in the praise thereof spends all his might,
To make me tongue-tied speaking of your fame.
But since your worth, wide as the ocean is,
The humble as the proudest sail doth bear,
My saucy bark, inferior far to his,
On your broad main doth willfully appear.
Your shallowest help will hold me up afloat,
Whilst he upon your soundless deep doth ride;
Or, being wracked, I am a worthless boat,
He of tall building and of goodly pride.
    Then, if he thrive and I be cast away,
    The worst was this: my love was my decay.

NO FEAR SHAKESPEARE

80

I get very discouraged when I write about you, knowing that a superior writer is writing about you too. He uses all of his powers of praise to make me tongue-tied when I write about your glory. But since your worth is as big as the ocean, able to support the smallest boat as well as the biggest ship, my impudent little boat, which is far inferior to his, stubbornly makes an appearance on your waters. Even at your shallowest, you keep me afloat, while he sails out over your measureless depths. And if I wind up being wrecked, I'm only a worthless little vessel, whereas he's a tall ship—something to be proud of. So if he does well and I find myself shipwrecked and discarded, the worst I can say is this: I was destroyed because of my love for you.

81

Or I shall live, your epitaph to make,
Or you survive, when I in earth am rotten,
From hence your memory death cannot take,
Although in me each part will be forgotten.
Your name from hence immortal life shall have,
Though I, once gone, to all the world must die.
The earth can yield me but a common grave,
When you entombèd in men's eyes shall lie.
Your monument shall be my gentle verse,
Which eyes not yet created shall o'er-read,
And tongues to be your being shall rehearse
When all the breathers of this world are dead.
    You still shall live—such virtue hath my pen—
    Where breath most breathes, ev'n in the mouths of men.

81

Either I will live to write your epitaph after you die, or you will survive me when I'm rotting in the grave. Death cannot take away your memory, but it will cause everything to do with *me* to be forgotten. Your name will live eternally, but once I'm gone, I'll be dead to the world. I'll only be granted an ordinary grave, but your tomb will be where everyone can see it. Your monument will be these tender poems of mine, which future generations will read and talk about, when everyone who's now living is dead. My pen has such power that you'll not only stay alive, you'll live where the essence of life resides: in the breath and voices of men.

82

I grant thou wert not married to my muse,
And therefore mayst without attaint o'erlook
The dedicated words which writers use
Of their fair subject, blessing every book.
Thou art as fair in knowledge as in hue,
Finding thy worth a limit past my praise,
And therefore art enforced to seek anew
Some fresher stamp of the time-bett'ring days.
And do so, love; yet when they have devised
What strainèd touches rhetoric can lend,
Thou, truly fair, wert truly sympathized
In true plain words by thy true-telling friend.
    And their gross painting might be better used
    Where cheeks need blood—in thee it is abused.

82

I admit that you weren't married to my poetry, so you're not doing anything wrong if you read what other writers say about you in the books they dedicate to you—you, the beautiful subject that blesses their books. You are as knowledgeable as you are beautiful, and you see that I'm incapable of praising you sufficiently, so you're forced to look again for some newer, fresher writer in these days of literary improvements. Go ahead and do so, my love. Yet while these writers have invented whatever elaborate stylistic devices they can borrow from rhetoric, you would be more truthfully represented, since you're truly beautiful, by the true, plain words of your truth-telling friend. And the overblown praise of these other writers might be more appropriately applied to people who *need* to be beautified. For you, such rhetorical excess is misused.

83

I never saw that you did painting need,
And therefore to your fair no painting set.
I found, or thought I found, you did exceed
The barren tender of a poet's debt.
And therefore have I slept in your report,
That you yourself, being extant, well might show
How far a modern quill doth come too short,
Speaking of worth, what worth in you doth grow.
This silence for my sin you did impute,
Which shall be most my glory, being dumb.
For I impair not beauty, being mute,
When others would give life, and bring a tomb.
   There lives more life in one of your fair eyes
   Than both your poets can in praise devise.

83

It never seemed to me that you needed to be praised, so I never described your beauty with profuse or elaborate rhetoric. I could see (or I thought I could see) that you were better than any praise a poet could give you. Therefore, I haven't exerted myself to describe you, so that you yourself, since you're still alive, could show everybody how much more worthy you are than my commonplace writing style can describe. You decided that this silence on my part was a fault, but I'm particularly proud of my muteness. By remaining silent, at least I don't damage your beauty, whereas other writers try to bring you to life in their writing, and kill you instead. You possess more life in one of your beautiful eyes than all of your poets could invent by praising you.

84

Who is it that says most, which can say more
Than this rich praise, that you alone are you—
In whose confíne immurèd is the store
Which should example where your equal grew?
Lean penury within that pen doth dwell
That to his subject lends not some small glory.
But he that writes of you, if he can tell
That you are you, so dignifies his story.
Let him but copy what in you is writ,
Not making worse what nature made so clear,
And such a counterpart shall fame his wit,
Making his style admired everywhere.
    You to your beauteous blessings add a curse,
    Being fond on praise, which makes your praises worse.

84

Which writer says the most about you? Which of them can say anything more to praise you than that only you are you, and that all beauty is stored in you, so that there's nothing to compare you to but yourself? Only a very poor writer is unable to improve the subject he's writing about at least a little, but whoever writes about you will have given his writing dignity simply by reporting that you are you. If that writer simply describes you accurately, managing not to mess up what nature made so perfectly, he'll have created such an image that his writing skills will become famous, his style admired everywhere. For all of the beauty you're blessed with, you curse yourself by loving to hear yourself praised so much, because then people write worse praise trying to flatter you.

85

My tongue-tied muse in manners holds her still,
While comments of your praise, richly compiled,
Reserve their character with golden quill
And precious phrase by all the muses filed.
I think good thoughts, whilst other write good words,
And like unlettered clerk still cry "Amen"
To every hymn that able spirit affords,
In polished form of well-refinèd pen.
Hearing you praised, I say "'Tis so, 'tis true,"
And to the most of praise add something more;
But that is in my thought, whose love to you,
Though words come hindmost, holds his rank before.
   Then others for the breath of words respect,
   Me for my dumb thoughts, speaking in effect.

85

My mute poetry politely remains silent, while commentaries praising you pile up, capturing the essence of your character in golden words and precious phrases inspired by all the muses. I think good thoughts about you while other people write good words, and like an illiterate parish clerk I continually cry "amen" to every poem of praise that capable poets produce about you in their polished and refined style. When I hear you praised, I say, "That's right, that's true," and add a little something to their utmost praise of you. What I add is only in my own mind, but in my own mind I know I love you the most, though I speak the least. So respect others for the words of praise they offer you, but respect me for my silent thoughts, which express themselves only in actions.

Parish clerks told the church congregation when to respond and when to say "amen" during services.

86

Was it the proud full sail of his great verse,
Bound for the prize of all too precious you,
That did my ripe thoughts in my brain inhearse,
Making their tomb the womb wherein they grew?
Was it his spirit, by spirits taught to write
Above a mortal pitch, that struck me dead?
No, neither he, nor his compeers by night
Giving him aid, my verse astonishèd.
He, nor that affable familiar ghost
Which nightly gulls him with intelligence,
As victors of my silence cannot boast.
I was not sick of any fear from thence;
    But when your countenance filled up his line,
    Then lacked I matter, that enfeebled mine.

NO FEAR SHAKESPEARE

86

Was it the ambitious and impressive poem that my rival wrote for you that discouraged me from writing my own poem, killing my thoughts before I could put them into words? Was it his creative power, aided by the spirits of all the dead authors he's read so that he writes better than any mortal should, that stunned me into silence? No, it was neither him nor those friends of his who visit him at night and help him, who silenced me with amazement. Neither he nor that friendly little ghost that tricks him with false information each night can boast that they're responsible for my silence. I wasn't sick because of any fear of them. But when you looked favorably on his writing and thus made it even better, then I suddenly had nothing to say, and you made my writing feeble.

The ghosts who visit the rival poet at night, both helping and tricking him, are very difficult to explain. They seem to refer to something in Shakespeare's time that is now unknown.

87

Farewell, thou art too dear for my possessing,
And like enough thou know'st thy estimate.
The charter of thy worth gives thee releasing;
My bonds in thee are all determinate.
For how do I hold thee but by thy granting,
And for that riches where is my deserving?
The cause of this fair gift in me is wanting,
And so my patent back again is swerving.
Thyself thou gav'st, thy own worth then not knowing,
Or me, to whom thou gav'st it, else mistaking;
So thy great gift, upon misprision growing,
Comes home again, on better judgment making.
   Thus have I had thee as a dream doth flatter:
   In sleep a king, but waking no such matter.

87

Goodbye; you're too valuable for me to hold onto, and you probably know exactly what you're worth. Your high value gives you the right to leave me; you have severed the ties that bind me to you. For what hold do I have over you except the hold that you choose to give me, and how do I deserve such a treasure? There's nothing in me to justify such a beautiful gift, so my right to possess you is reverting back to you. When you gave yourself to me, you didn't know your own worth, or else you were mistaken about me, the person you gave yourself to. So the great gift you gave me, being based on a false estimate, goes back to you now that you're able to make a better judgment. Thus, the time in which I had you was like a flattering dream; while I was asleep, I thought I was a king, but when I woke up, I found that was not the case.

88

When thou shalt be disposed to set me light
And place my merit in the eye of scorn,
Upon thy side against myself I'll fight,
And prove thee virtuous, though thou art forsworn.
With mine own weakness being best acquainted,
Upon thy part I can set down a story
Of faults concealed, wherein I am attainted,
That thou in losing me shalt win much glory.
And I by this will be a gainer too,
For bending all my loving thoughts on thee,
The injuries that to myself I do,
Doing thee vantage, double vantage me.
   Such is my love, to thee I so belong,
   That for thy right myself will bear all wrong.

88

When you feel inclined to think little of me and make other people scorn me, I'll take your side and argue against myself, demonstrating that you're virtuous even while you're lying about me. Since I know my own weaknesses better than anyone, I can tell a story about my hidden faults (in which I reveal myself as morally tainted) that will have people thinking better of you for not being with me anymore. And I, too, will gain by turning all my loving thoughts to you: Whatever injuries I do to myself will help you, which will help me doubly. I love you so much—belong to you so totally—that to get you everything you're entitled to, I will take every wrong upon myself.

89

Say that thou didst forsake me for some fault,
And I will comment upon that offense.
Speak of my lameness, and I straight will halt,
Against thy reasons making no defense.
Thou canst not, love, disgrace me half so ill,
To set a form upon desired change,
As I'll myself disgrace, knowing thy will;
I will acquaintance strangle and look strange,
Be absent from thy walks, and in my tongue
Thy sweet belovèd name no more shall dwell,
Lest I, too much profane, should do it wrong
And haply of our old acquaintance tell.
   For thee against myself I'll vow debate,
   For I must ne'er love him whom thou dost hate.

89

(Continuing from Sonnet 88) If you tell people you left me because of some fault of mine, I will expand upon whatever you say I did wrong. Say I'm lame, and I'll start limping immediately, without trying to defend myself against your accusations. My love, in finding a reason to justify leaving me, you can't disgrace me half as badly as I'll disgrace myself, as soon as I know what you want. I'll pretend I don't know you and act like a stranger. I won't go where I might run into you. And I won't mention your beloved name anymore in case I'd dirty it by reminding people that we used to be acquainted. For your sake, I'll vow to be my own enemy, because I must not love someone whom you hate.

90

Then hate me when thou wilt, if ever, now,
Now while the world is bent my deeds to cross;
Join with the spite of fortune, make me bow,
And do not drop in for an after-loss:
Ah, do not, when my heart hath 'scaped this sorrow,
Come in the rearward of a conquered woe.
Give not a windy night a rainy morrow,
To linger out a purposed overthrow.
If thou wilt leave me, do not leave me last,
When other petty griefs have done their spite
But in the onset come; so shall I taste
At first the very worst of fortune's might;
    And other strains of woe, which now seem woe,
    Compared with loss of thee will not seem so.

90

(Continuing from Sonnet 89) So hate me when you want to, but if you're ever going to, do it now, now while the world is determined to frustrate everything I try to do. Add to my misfortune, make me collapse under it, don't hit me with this later, after I've already endured so many other blows. Ah, do not let me think I've avoided the sorrow of losing you, then come and reject me—right after I've been defeated by another grief. Don't turn my windy night into a rainy tomorrow, prolonging the defeat you intend to give me. If you're going to leave me, don't wait until the end, after other little sorrows have done their damage. Leave me at the beginning, so I experience the worst misfortune first. Then other hurtful things, which seem painful now, won't seem so, compared with losing you.

91

Some glory in their birth, some in their skill,
Some in their wealth, some in their body's force,
Some in their garments, though new-fangled ill,
Some in their hawks and hounds, some in their horse;
And every humor hath his adjunct pleasure,
Wherein it finds a joy above the rest.
But these particulars are not my measure;
All these I better in one general best.
Thy love is better than high birth to me,
Richer than wealth, prouder than garments' cost,
Of more delight than hawks or horses be;
And having thee, of all men's pride I boast;
   Wretched in this alone, that thou mayst take
   All this away, and me most wretched make.

91

Some people are proud of the social status they've inherited; some people of their abilities; some of their wealth; some of how strong they are; some of their clothes, though the clothes are trendy and weird; some are proud of their hawks and hounds; some of their horses; and every individual temperament has its particular pleasure, something the person enjoys above everything else. But I don't measure happiness by any of these things. There's something else that's better than them all. To me, your love is better than high social status, more valuable than wealth, more worth being proud of than expensive clothes, and more enjoyable than hawks or horses. And having you, I have something better than what other men are proud of—except I'm wretched in this one respect: You can take all this away from me and make me completely wretched.

92

But do thy worst to steal thyself away,
For term of life thou art assurèd mine,
And life no longer than thy love will stay,
For it depends upon that love of thine.
Then need I not to fear the worst of wrongs,
When in the least of them my life hath end.
I see a better state to me belongs
Than that which on thy humor doth depend.
Thou canst not vex me with inconstant mind,
Since that my life on thy revolt doth lie.
O what a happy title do I find,
Happy to have thy love, happy to die!
    But what's so blessèd-fair that fears no blot?
    Thou mayst be false, and yet I know it not.

NO FEAR SHAKESPEARE

92

(Continuing from Sonnet 91) But go ahead and leave me—do your best to hurt me. I'm sure to have you as long as I'm alive, because I will only be alive as long as you love me: My life depends on your love. Now I don't have to worry about all the terrible things you might do to hurt me; as soon as you hurt me even a little, I'll die. I realize now that I'm in a better position than I would be if I were dependent on your affections. You can't worry me with the idea that you're fickle, since my life would be over as soon as you changed your mind about me. Oh, what a happy position I'm in: I'm happy to have your love, but also happy to die! But what situation is so perfectly blessed that it breeds no worries? You might be unfaithful to me without my knowing it.

93

So shall I live, supposing thou art true,
Like a deceived husband; so love's face
May still seem love to me, though altered new:
Thy looks with me, thy heart in other place.
For there can live no hatred in thine eye,
Therefore in that I cannot know thy change.
In many's looks, the false heart's history
Is writ in moods and frowns and wrinkles strange,
But heav'n in thy creation did decree
That in thy face sweet love should ever dwell;
Whate'er thy thoughts or thy heart's workings be,
Thy looks should nothing thence but sweetness tell.
   How like Eve's apple doth thy beauty grow,
   If thy sweet virtue answer not thy show.

93

(Continuing from Sonnet 92) In that case, I'll live like a deceived husband, assuming you're faithful. Then your face will still show that you love me, even though you don't—your looks will stay the same, but your heart will be somewhere else. As your face could never have a hateful expression, I couldn't ever know a change of heart from looking at it. Many people express their unfaithfulness in their faces—in moody looks and frowns and strange wrinkles. But when heaven created you, it decided that your face would always express sweet love. Whatever your thoughts or desires, your looks never express anything but sweetness. In fact, your beauty becomes much like Eve's apple when you're not as sweet and virtuous as you look.

94

They that have pow'r to hurt, and will do none,
That do not do the thing they most do show,
Who moving others are themselves as stone,
Unmovèd, cold, and to temptation slow,
They rightly do inherit heaven's graces,
And husband nature's riches from expense.
They are the lords and owners of their faces;
Others but stewards of their excellence.
The summer's flow'r is to the summer sweet,
Though to itself it only live and die.
But if that flow'r with base infection meet,
The basest weed outbraves his dignity.
   For sweetest things turn sourest by their deeds;
   Lilies that fester smell far worse than weeds.

94

Those whose beauty gives them the power to hurt others, but who refuse to; those who look very sexy but won't have sex; who attract other people but are themselves like stones—cold, unemotional, and difficult to tempt—those are the ones who will rightly inherit heaven's blessings and keep nature's treasures from being wasted. Those who have self-control truly own their beauty; the rest are only administering their beauty for others' use. The summer flower seems sweet to us in summer, though the flower itself may feel that it's only living and dying. But if that flower lets itself be infected by a parasite, the lowest weed will be better, for the sweetest things have the capacity to turn the sourest by acting wrongly. Lilies that rot smell a lot worse than weeds.

95

How sweet and lovely dost thou make the shame
Which, like a canker in the fragrant rose,
Doth spot the beauty of thy budding name!
O in what sweets dost thou thy sins enclose!
That tongue that tells the story of thy days,
Making lascivious comments on thy sport,
Cannot dispraise but in a kind of praise;
Naming thy name blesses an ill report.
O what a mansion have those vices got
Which for their habitation chose out thee,
Where beauty's veil doth cover every blot,
And all things turns to fair that eyes can see!
   Take heed, dear heart, of this large privilege;
   The hardest knife ill used doth lose his edge.

NO FEAR SHAKESPEARE

95

You make the flaw that's ruining your reputation (like a worm infecting a rosebud) look so sweet and lovely. Oh, you cover up your sins with such a sweet exterior! The person who accuses you of wild lust somehow manages to turn his criticisms into praise: Your name makes bad actions look good. Oh, the vices you have inside you live in a beautiful house. Your beauty serves as a veil that makes every bad thing you do seem good! But be careful, dear heart, with this great privilege that your beauty gives you. If you abuse it, it will stop working, like a knife that loses its edge from misuse.

96

Some say thy fault is youth, some wantonness,
Some say thy grace is youth and gentle sport;
Both grace and faults are loved of more and less;
Thou mak'st faults graces that to thee resort.
As on the finger of a thronèd queen
The basest jewel will be well esteemed,
So are those errors that in thee are seen
To truths translated, and for true things deemed.
How many lambs might the stern wolf betray,
If like a lamb he could his looks translate;
How many gazers mightst thou lead away,
If thou wouldst use the strength of all thy state!
   But do not so. I love thee in such sort,
   As thou being mine, mine is thy good report.

96

Some say your fault is your youth, others that the problem is your lustfulness. Some say your youth and playfulness are charming. Both important and unimportant people love your charms and your faults too. You turn your faults into sources of charm. Just as a worthless jewel is regarded as valuable when a queen is wearing it, so the sins that people see you commit are turned into good characteristics and regarded as good. How many lambs could the grim wolf trick if he could make himself look like a lamb? How many people might you lead astray if you seduced them with the full force of your beauty and social position? But don't do that. I love you so much (since you are mine) that your reputation extends to me as well.

97

How like a winter hath my absence been
From thee, the pleasure of the fleeting year!
What freezings have I felt, what dark days seen!
What old December's bareness everywhere!
And yet this time removed was summer's time,
The teeming autumn big with rich increase,
Bearing the wanton burthen of the prime,
Like widowed wombs after their lords' decease.
Yet this abundant issue seemed to me
But hope of orphans, and unfathered fruit.
For summer and his pleasures wait on thee,
And thou away, the very birds are mute.
    Or if they sing, 'tis with so dull a cheer
    That leaves look pale, dreading the winter's near.

97

My separation from you has felt just like winter, since you're what makes the year pleasurable! I've felt very cold, and the days have seemed very dark, and everything has been as barren as in December! And yet the time we've been apart was actually summer, then fall, the harvest-time when nature gives birth to crops planted in the spring like a woman giving birth after her husband has died. And these abundant fruits of nature seemed like hopeless orphans to me, because summer and summer's pleasures all depend on you, and, with you away, even the birds are silent. Or if they sing, they do it so dismally that the leaves grow pale with fear, dreading the fact that winter's almost here.

The speaker personifies the spring as a dead father because the season is gone even while the crops planted during its duration remain.

98

From you have I been absent in the spring,
When proud-pied April, dressed in all his trim,
Hath put a spirit of youth in everything,
That heavy Saturn laughed and leapt with him.
Yet nor the lays of birds, nor the sweet smell
Of different flow'rs in odor and in hue,
Could make me any summer's story tell,
Or from their proud lap pluck them where they grew.
Nor did I wonder at the lily's white,
Nor praise the deep vermilion in the rose;
They were but sweet, but figures of delight,
Drawn after you, you pattern of all those.
    Yet seemed it winter still, and, you away,
    As with your shadow I with these did play.

98

I was away from you during the spring, when splendid April in all its finery made everything feel so young that even Saturn, the god of old age and gloominess, laughed and leaped along with it. But neither the songs of birds nor the sweet smell of all the various flowers could make me feel like it was summer or inspire me to go flower picking. I wasn't amazed by how white the lily was, nor did I praise the deep red of the roses. They were only sweet, only pictures of delight, drawn in imitation of you, the archetype of spring. It seemed like it was still winter and, with you away, I played with these flowers as if I were playing with your reflection.

99

The forward violet thus did I chide:
Sweet thief, whence didst thou steal thy sweet that smells,
If not from my love's breath? The purple pride
Which on thy soft cheek for complexion dwells
In my love's veins thou hast too grossly dyed.
The lily I condemnèd for thy hand,
And buds of marjoram had stol'n thy hair;
The roses fearfully on thorns did stand,
One blushing shame, another white despair;
A third, nor red nor white, had stol'n of both,
And to his robb'ry had annexed thy breath;
But for his theft, in pride of all his growth
A vengeful canker ate him up to death.
   More flow'rs I noted, yet I none could see
   But sweet or color it had stol'n from thee.

99

(Continuing from Sonnet 98) This is how I scolded the presumptuous violet: "Sweet thief, where did you steal your sweet smell from if not from my beloved's breath? You obviously got that purple color you're so proud of by dying yourself in his blood." I condemned the lily for stealing its whiteness from your hand and the marjoram buds for stealing your curly hair. The roses stood by anxiously, the red one blushing in shame, the white one pale with despair, knowing they were guilty of stealing your colors too. A third rose, neither red nor white, had stolen both red and white from your complexion, and added to his robbery the smell of your breath. But as punishment for his theft, a vengeful worm destroyed the rose just at its proudest growth. I noticed other flowers, and I couldn't see any that hadn't stolen its sweetness or color from you.

100

Where art thou, Muse, that thou forget'st so long
To speak of that which gives thee all thy might?
Spend'st thou thy fury on some worthless song,
Dark'ning thy pow'r to lend base subjects light?
Return, forgetful Muse, and straight redeem
In gentle numbers time so idly spent;
Sing to the ear that doth thy lays esteem,
And gives thy pen both skill and argument.
Rise, resty Muse; my love's sweet face survey,
If time have any wrinkle graven there;
If any, be a satire to decay,
And make time's spoils despisèd everywhere.
   Give my love fame faster than time wastes life;
   So thou prevent'st his scythe and crookèd knife.

100

Where have you been, Muse, that you have forgotten for so long to inspire me to write about the person who gives you all your power? Are you using up your inspiration on some worthless poem, eclipsing your true powers by making unworthy topics seem brighter? Return, forgetful Muse, and make up for the time you've wasted by inspiring me to write some gentle verses. Inspire poems addressed to my beloved, the person who actually likes your songs, and who gives you both poetic skill and a topic to write about. Get up, sleepy Muse: Examine my beloved's sweet face to see if time has engraved any wrinkles on it. If there are any, then satirize aging and make everybody despise time's destructive powers. Make my beloved famous faster than time can destroy his life; prevent time's knife from cutting my beloved down.

101

O truant Muse, what shall be thy amends
For thy neglect of truth in beauty dyed?
Both truth and beauty on my love depends;
So dost thou too, and therein dignified.
Make answer, Muse: wilt thou not haply say
Truth needs no color, with his color fixed,
Beauty no pencil, beauty's truth to lay;
But best is best if never intermixed?
Because he needs no praise, wilt thou be dumb?
Excuse not silence so, for 't lies in thee
To make him much outlive a gilded tomb,
And to be praised of ages yet to be.
    Then do thy office, Muse. I teach thee how
    To make him seem long hence as he shows now.

NO FEAR SHAKESPEARE

101

(Continuing from Sonnet 100) Oh truant Muse, how are you going to make amends for neglecting my beloved, the embodiment of truth bound up with beauty? Both truth and beauty depend upon my beloved. You depend on, and are dignified by, him too. Answer me, Muse; perhaps you'll say, "Truth doesn't need to be embellished when it's already attached to beauty. Beauty doesn't need to be poetically described in order for its truth to be apparent. Whatever is best is best when it's not mixed with anything else." But just because my beloved needs no praise, will you be silent? You can't excuse this silence, as you have the ability to make him live longer than a golden tomb and win the praise of future ages. Then do your job, Muse. I'll teach you how to make him look in the distant future like he does now.

102

My love is strengthened, though more weak in seeming;
I love not less, though less the show appear.
That love is merchandised whose rich esteeming
The owner's tongue doth publish everywhere.
Our love was new, and then but in the spring,
When I was wont to greet it with my lays,
As Philomel in summer's front doth sing,
And stops his pipe in growth of riper days.
Not that the summer is less pleasant now
Than when her mournful hymns did hush the night,
But that wild music burthens every bough,
And sweets grown common lose their dear delight.
    Therefore, like her, I sometime hold my tongue,
    Because I would not dull you with my song.

102

My love is stronger, though it seems weaker. I don't love less, but I show my love less. When a person broadcasts how he loves and how richly he esteems the person he loves, he turns his love into a commodity. Our love was still new when I used to write poems about it, just as the nightingale sings at the beginning of summer, then stops singing as the summer progresses. It's not that summer is less pleasant now than the nights when the nightingale sang. It's just that every tree branch is filled with songbirds, and when things are common they're less delightful. Therefore, like the nightingale, sometimes I keep silent because I don't want to bore you with my song.

103

Alack, what poverty my muse brings forth,
That having such a scope to show her pride,
The argument all bare is of more worth
Than when it hath my added praise beside!
O blame me not if I no more can write!
Look in your glass, and there appears a face
That overgoes my blunt invention quite,
Dulling my lines and doing me disgrace.
Were it not sinful then, striving to mend,
To mar the subject that before was well?
For to no other pass my verses tend
Than of your graces and your gifts to tell;
   And more, much more than in my verse can sit
   Your own glass shows you, when you look in it.

103

Alas, I'm a poor poet, since even with such a great subject to write about (you), the subject is worth more by itself than with my praise added to it. Don't blame me if I can't write anymore! Look in the mirror, and you'll see a face that quite overwhelms my limited poetic skills, making my lines stupid and thereby disgracing me. It would be a sin, wouldn't it, if in trying to improve my poetry, I messed up their subject, which was perfectly fine before? For the only things I write about are your charms and your wonderful qualities, and your own mirror will show you far, far more of these than I can possibly fit into my poetry.

104

To me, fair friend, you never can be old,
For as you were when first your eye I eyed,
Such seems your beauty still. Three winters cold
Have from the forests shook three summers' pride;
Three beauteous springs to yellow autumn turned
In process of the seasons have I seen;
Three April pérfumes in three hot Junes burned,
Since first I saw you fresh, which yet are green.
Ah yet doth beauty, like a dial hand,
Steal from his figure, and no pace perceived;
So your sweet hue, which methinks still doth stand,
Hath motion, and mine eye may be deceived.
   For fear of which, hear this, thou age unbred:
   Ere you were born was beauty's summer dead.

104

You'll never be old to me, beautiful friend, for your beauty seems just the same as it was when I first saw your lovely eyes. Since then, three cold winters have stripped the leaves off three proud summers; three beautiful springs have turned to three yellow autumns, all in the course of the seasons. Three Aprils, full of perfumed flowers, have all burned up into three hot Junes since the first day I saw you in your freshness—and you're still fresh and green. Ah, but beauty, like the hand of a clock, creeps away from the person it's attached to so slowly no one can see it. In the same way, your sweet beauty, which seems to be standing still, is actually changing, and my eye may be deceived. In case it is, hear this, future generations: Before you were born, the greatest example of beauty was already dead.

105

Let not my love be called idolatry,
Nor my belovèd as an idol show,
Since all alike my songs and praises be
To one, of one, still such, and ever so.
Kind is my love today, tomorrow kind,
Still constant in a wondrous excellence;
Therefore my verse to constancy confined,
One thing expressing, leaves out difference.
Fair, kind, and true is all my argument,
Fair, kind, and true, varying to other words;
And in this change is my invention spent—
Three themes in one, which wondrous scope affords.
   Fair, kind, and true have often lived alone,
   Which three, till now, never kept seat in one.

NO FEAR SHAKESPEARE

105

The humor of this sonnet is that while defending himself against the charge of idolatry, the speaker echoes language traditionally used by Christians to describe God.

Let no one call my love idolatry or say that I treat my beloved as an idol, since all of my poems and praises have been addressed to one person, are about one person, and always will be. My love is kind today, will be kind tomorrow, always constant in wondrous excellence. Therefore, since my poetry is confined to a subject that's always the same, it always expresses the same thing, never including anything different. The subject of my poems is the beautiful, kind, and faithful. I write about the beautiful, kind, and faithful in various ways, and this is the task that I expend all of my creativity on—three themes rolled up in one person, which offers an amazing scope for poetic invention. Beauty, kindness, and fidelity have often been divided into different people, but the three of them were never together in one person until now.

106

When in the chronicle of wasted time
I see descriptions of the fairest wights
And beauty making beautiful old rhyme
In praise of ladies dead and lovely knights,
Then in the blazon of sweet beauty's best,
Of hand, of foot, of lip, of eye, of brow,
I see their ántique pen would have expressed
Ev'n such a beauty as you master now.
So all their praises are but prophecies
Of this our time, all you prefiguring,
And for they looked but with divining eyes,
They had not skill enough your worth to sing.
   For we which now behold these present days,
   Have eyes to wonder, but lack tongues to praise.

106

When in accounts of historic times I come upon descriptions of very beautiful people and read the beautiful poems inspired by them, in praise of ladies now dead and lovely knights; when I see the poems catalog their beauty—their hands, feet, lips, eyes, foreheads—I realize that these ancient writers were trying to describe the same kind of beauty that you possess now. So all the praises of these writers are actually prophecies of our time; all of them prefigure you. If the writers hadn't been divinely inspired with this gift of prophecy, they wouldn't have had the skill to describe your worth. Those of us who live now may be able to see your beauty firsthand and be amazed by it, but we lack the poetic skill to describe it.

107

Not mine own fears, nor the prophetic soul
Of the wide world dreaming on things to come,
Can yet the lease of my true love control,
Supposed as forfeit to a cónfined doom.
The mortal moon hath her eclipse endured
And the sad augurs mock their own preságe;
Incertainties now crown themselves assured,
And peace proclaims olives of endless age.
Now with the drops of this most balmy time
My love looks fresh, and death to me subscribes,
Since spite of him I'll live in this poor rhyme,
While he insults o'er dull and speechless tribes.
   And thou in this shalt find thy monument,
   When tyrants' crests and tombs of brass are spent.

NO FEAR SHAKESPEARE

107

This sonnet is puzzling because it seems to refer to actual events in Shakespeare's time, but it's impossible to know for certain which events it refers to. One possibility is that it alludes to Queen Elizabeth's death (represented by the moon's eclipse, described in line 5) and the subsequent release from prison of the earl of Southampton, whom some readers believe to be the young man of the sonnets. However, even in Shakespeare's time, this sonnet was probably somewhat mysterious.

Neither my own fears nor the speculations of the rest of the world about the future can continue to keep me from possessing my beloved, who everybody thought was doomed to remain in prison. The moon, which was always mortal, has finally been eclipsed, and the gloomy fortune-tellers now laugh at their own predictions. Things that once seemed doubtful have become certainties, and peace has come to stay. Now, with the blessings of these times, my beloved looks fresh again and death itself submits to me, since in spite of death I'll live on in this poor poem while death only exults over the stupid and illiterate peoples that he's overcome. And you will find this poem to be your monument when tyrants reach the end of their reigns and tombs of brass fall into decay.

108

What's in the brain that ink may character
Which hath not figured to thee my true spirit?
What's new to speak, what now to register,
That may express my love or thy dear merit?
Nothing, sweet boy; but yet, like prayers divine,
I must each day say o'er the very same,
Counting no old thing old, thou mine, I thine,
Ev'n as when first I hallowed thy fair name.
So that eternal love in love's fresh case
Weighs not the dust and injury of age,
Nor gives to necessary wrinkles place,
But makes antiquity for aye his page,
    Finding the first conceit of love there bred
    Where time and outward form would show it dead.

NO FEAR SHAKESPEARE

108

What could I possibly write that I haven't written already to show you how constant and faithful my soul is? What else is there to say, what new thing can I invent, that would express either my love or your value? There's nothing, sweet boy. And yet, just as with prayers to God, I have to keep saying the same thing over and over again each day, without thinking that these old praises are old. You're mine, I'm yours, just like when I first honored your name in writing. My love for you, which is everlasting, doesn't care about the effects of age, nor does it acknowledge your wrinkles, but always inspires me to describe my feelings as if they were still young. I see in you the original source of my love for you, even though your age and appearance would suggest that the reason for that love is dead.

109

O never say that I was false of heart,
Though absence seemed my flame to qualify.
As easy might I from myself depart
As from my soul, which in thy breast doth lie.
That is my home of love; if I have ranged,
Like him that travels I return again,
Just to the time, not with the time exchanged,
So that myself bring water for my stain.
Never believe, though in my nature reigned
All frailties that besiege all kinds of blood,
That it could so preposterously be stained
To leave for nothing all thy sum of good.
   For nothing this wide universe I call,
   Save thou, my rose; in it thou art my all.

NO FEAR SHAKESPEARE

109

Oh, never say that I was unfaithful to you in my heart, even though my absence from you suggested that my love had weakened. I can't separate myself from my feelings for you anymore than I can separate myself from myself. You are my home, and if I strayed away from you, like a traveler I have returned again, right at the appointed time, with my feelings unchanged, so I'm making up for my misdeed. Even though I have the same weaknesses in my nature as everyone made of flesh and blood, don't ever believe that I could be so morally compromised as to leave someone as good as you in exchange for something worthless. The entire universe except for you, my love, means nothing to me. You're everything to me.

110

Alas 'tis true, I have gone here and there,
And made myself a motley to the view,
Gored mine own thoughts, sold cheap what is most dear,
Made old offenses of affections new.
Most true it is that I have looked on truth
Askance and strangely; but by all above,
These blenches gave my heart another youth,
And worse essays proved thee my best of love.
Now all is done, save what shall have no end;
Mine appetite I never more will grind
On newer proof, to try an older friend,
A god in love, to whom I am confined.
    Then give me welcome, next my heav'n the best,
    Ev'n to thy pure and most most loving breast.

NO FEAR SHAKESPEARE

110

Alas, it's true, I have gone here and there, and made myself look foolish, and allowed my thoughts to be divided, and acted as if the most valuable thing were worthless, and used my new friends to commit the old infidelities I've committed before. It's very true that I've treated true love strangely and with disdain. But I swear by heaven, these moments when I've swerved aside have made my heart young again, and by trying out other people I've proved to myself that you're the best person I love. Now I've finished with everything except for our love, which will have no end. I will no longer whet my appetite for new lovers, causing suffering to my old friend, the god of love to whom I'm now limiting myself. So welcome me back into your pure and loving heart; to me, you're the next best thing to heaven.

111

O for my sake do you with Fortune chide,
The guilty goddess of my harmful deeds,
That did not better for my life provide
Than public means which public manners breeds.
Thence comes it that my name receives a brand,
And almost thence my nature is subdued
To what it works in, like the dyer's hand:
Pity me then, and wish I were renewed,
Whilst like a willing patient I will drink
Potions of eisel 'gainst my strong infection;
No bitterness that I will bitter think,
Nor double penance, to correct correction.
    Pity me then, dear friend, and I assure ye,
    Ev'n that your pity is enough to cure me.

111

The speaker's reference to his public profession is usually interpreted as referring to Shakespeare's profession as an actor.

I know you curse my bad luck for having no better way to make a living than in front of the public, which has had a bad effect on my morals and behavior. This is why I have a bad name, and coming into contact with the public so much has polluted my very nature, just like a cloth-dyer's hand becomes stained with his dye. So take pity on me and hope that I can go back to being the way I would have been if I hadn't been contaminated by the public; meanwhile, I'll drink bitter medicines made of vinegar to cure myself of this infection. I won't think that the medicine's bitter no matter how bitter it is, nor will I protest at having to do double penance to try to undo the bad influence. So pity me, dear friend, and I assure you: Your pity alone is enough to cure me.

112

Your love and pity doth th' impression fill
Which vulgar scandal stamped upon my brow;
For what care I who calls me well or ill,
So you o'er-green my bad, my good allow?
You are my all the world, and I must strive
To know my shames and praises from your tongue;
None else to me, nor I to none alive,
That my steeled sense or changes right or wrong.
In so profound abysm I throw all care
Of others' voices, that my adder's sense
To critic and to flatt'rer stoppèd are.
Mark how with my neglect I do dispense:
    You are so strongly in my purpose bred
    That all the world besides methinks y'are dead.

112

(Continuing from Sonnet 111) Your love and pity make up for the damage popular opinion has done to my reputation, since what do I care who calls me good or bad as long as *you* gloss over what's bad about me and acknowledge my good? You're the entire world to me, and I have to strive to learn what's good or bad about me from what you say. No one else matters to me, and I matter to no one else alive. *Your opinion is so powerful with me that it determines what's right and wrong.* I care so little about what other people say that it's as if I threw their voices into a bottomless pit—that's how deaf I am to their flattery and criticism. Notice how I disregard the fact that the rest of the world neglects me. You matter so much to me that you're dead to the rest of the world.

Editors are unsure what line 8 actually means. The italicized translation represents this editor's best guess.

113

Since I left you, mine eye is in my mind,
And that which governs me to go about
Doth part his function, and is partly blind,
Seems seeing, but effectually is out;
For it no form delivers to the heart
Of bird, of flow'r, or shape which it doth latch.
Of his quick objects hath the mind no part,
Nor his own vision holds what it doth catch;
For if it see the rud'st or gentlest sight,
The most sweet favor or deformèd'st creature,
The mountain, or the sea, the day, or night,
The crow, or dove, it shapes them to your feature.
    Incapable of more, replete with you,
    My most true mind thus makes mine untrue.

113

Since I left you, I'm so absorbed in my own thoughts that I partly see where I'm going and partly don't. For my vision doesn't focus on the shapes of birds or flowers or anything else it lands on. My mind simply isn't on the living things that my eyes show it, nor do I remember the things I see. For whether I see the rudest or gentlest sight, the sweetest-looking or the most deformed creature, the mountain or the sea, the day or the night, the crow or the dove, my vision shapes them so they look like you. Incapable of seeing anything else and filled with your image, my faithfulness to you is making me see everything wrongly.

114

Or whether doth my mind, being crowned with you,
Drink up the monarch's plague, this flattery?
Or whether shall I say mine eye saith true,
And that your love taught it this alchemy,
To make of monsters and things indigest
Such cherubins as your sweet self resemble,
Creating every bad a perfect best
As fast as objects to his beams assemble?
O 'tis the first; 'tis flattery in my seeing,
And my great mind most kingly drinks it up.
Mine eye well knows what with his gust is greeing,
And to his palate doth prepare the cup.
  If it be poisoned, 'tis the lesser sin
  That mine eye loves it and doth first begin.

114

(Continuing from Sonnet 113) Is it the case that my mind, flattered by your love, has become susceptible to pleasurable delusions? Or is it the case that my eyes are seeing accurately, and my love for you has given me magical powers to turn monsters and shapeless things into angels that look like your sweet self, transforming every bad sight into the best and most perfect thing as fast as it comes into my field of vision? Oh, the first is true: My eyes are deluded, and my mind accepts these delusions like a king accepts flattery. My eye knows perfectly well what I like to see, and it shows me what it knows I'll enjoy. Though its visions are poisoned by falsehood, my eye can be partially excused by the fact that it likes these false visions too and consumes them first, like a servant who tastes the king's food to see if it's poisoned.

115

Those lines that I before have writ do lie,
Ev'n those that said I could not love you dearer.
Yet then my judgment knew no reason why
My most full flame should afterwards burn clearer.
But reck'ning time, whose millioned accidents
Creep in 'twixt vows, and change decrees of kings,
Tan sacred beauty, blunt the sharp'st intents,
Divert strong minds to the course of alt'ring things.
Alas, why, fearing of time's tyranny,
Might I not then say, "Now I love you best,"
When I was certain o'er incertainty,
Crowning the present, doubting of the rest?
  Love is a babe; then might I not say so,
  To give full growth to that which still doth grow?

115

I lied in those poems I wrote before where I said I couldn't love you any more than I did already. Back then I had no reason to think that my love, which was already burning intensely, could burn any brighter. Instead, I was depending on the fact that the passage of time—together with the millions of unexpected events that can come between lovers' promises and change even the decrees of kings—might darken a lover's sacred beauty, take the edge off of a lover's keenest intentions, and force the strongest minds to adapt to changing circumstances. Alas, why didn't I say back then, when I was worried about time's destructive power, "I love you best now"? I was so certain of my feelings despite the uncertainty, and I was ready to say my present happiness was complete, though I had doubts about everything to come. Love itself is a baby, so wouldn't it have been natural for me to have said that my love for you was fully grown, though it keeps growing?

"Love itself is a baby": Cupid, the god of love, was traditionally depicted as a baby boy.

116

Let me not to the marriage of true minds
Admit impediments. Love is not love
Which alters when it alteration finds,
Or bends with the remover to remove.
O no, it is an ever-fixèd mark
That looks on tempests and is never shaken;
It is the star to every wand'ring bark,
Whose worth's unknown, although his height be taken.
Love's not time's fool, though rosy lips and cheeks
Within his bending sickle's compass come:
Love alters not with his brief hours and weeks,
But bears it out even to the edge of doom.
   If this be error and upon me proved,
   I never writ, nor no man ever loved.

NO FEAR SHAKESPEARE

116

I hope I may never acknowledge any reason why minds that truly love each other shouldn't be joined together. Love isn't really love if it changes when it sees the beloved change or if it disappears when the beloved leaves. Oh no, love is a constant and unchanging light that shines on storms without being shaken; it is the star that guides every wandering boat. And like a star, its value is beyond measure, though its height can be measured. Love is not under time's power, though time has the power to destroy rosy lips and cheeks. Love does not alter with the passage of brief hours and weeks, but lasts until Doomsday. If I'm wrong about this and can be proven wrong, I never wrote, and no man ever loved.

117

Accuse me thus: that I have scanted all
Wherein I should your great deserts repay,
Forgot upon your dearest love to call,
Whereto all bonds do tie me day by day;
That I have frequent been with unknown minds,
And giv'n to time your own dear purchased right;
That I have hoisted sail to all the winds
Which should transport me farthest from your sight.
Book both my willfulness and errors down,
And on just proof surmise accumulate.
Bring me within the level of your frown,
But shoot not at me in your wakened hate,
    Since my appeal says I did strive to prove
    The constancy and virtue of your love.

117

Accuse me like this: Say that I've neglected every opportunity to repay the great obligation I owe you; that I've forgotten to invoke your precious love, though every day I'm more and more bound to you. Say that I've spent too much time with strangers, giving away the time that you have a right to spend with me. Say that I've let every wind blow me as far away as possible from you. Write a list of all the stubborn and wrong things I've done, and put together a lot of speculations about my other misdeeds based on what you already know. Get ready to frown at me, but don't frown at me because of what I've done to awaken new hatred in you, since I did it all to test the constancy and strength of your love.

118

Like as to make our appetites more keen
With eager compounds we our palate urge;
As, to prevent our maladies unseen,
We sicken to shun sickness when we purge;
Ev'n so, being full of your ne'er-cloying sweetness,
To bitter sauces did I frame my feeding;
And, sick of welfare, found a kind of meetness
To be diseased ere that there was true needing.
Thus policy in love, t' anticipate
The ills that were not, grew to faults assured,
And brought to medicine a healthful state
Which, rank of goodness, would by ill be cured;
   But thence I learn, and find the lesson true,
   Drugs poison him that so fell sick of you.

118

Just as we like to sharpen our appetites by eating pungent combinations of food or make ourselves vomit in order to ward off future illness, so, in the same way, because I was so full of your sweetness (not that it's ever cloying), I decided to switch from you to a more bitter diet. And because I was tired of being so healthy, I decided it would be good to make myself sick, using other people to keep from getting sick of you. With this wise relationship strategy, which I adopted in anticipation of problems that didn't exist, I actually became used to cheating on you. I applied medicine to a relationship that was healthy to begin with, attempting to cure something totally good by applying evil to it. But I learned from this—and I think what I learned is true—that the drugs I used are poisonous to me, since I'm so lovesick over you.

This is a reference to the Renaissance practice of "purging," which was thought to be healthy.

119

What potions have I drunk of siren tears,
Distilled from limbecks foul as hell within,
Applying fears to hopes, and hopes to fears,
Still losing when I saw myself to win!
What wretched errors hath my heart committed,
Whilst it hath thought itself so blessèd never!
How have mine eyes out of their spheres been fitted
In the distraction of this madding fever!
O benefit of ill, now I find true
That better is by evil still made better;
And ruined love when it is built anew
Grows fairer than at first, more strong, far greater.
  So I return rebuked to my content,
  And gain by ills thrice more than I have spent.

119

(Continuing from Sonnet 118) I've given myself medicines that seemed seductively sweet but in reality were foul as hell. I forced myself to doubt the things I was hopeful about and to be hopeful about what I should have worried about, always losing just when I expected myself to win! My heart committed wretched errors right at the moment when I thought I had never been more blessed! My eyes have popped out of their sockets in the delirium of this fever! But, oh, the benefits that evil brings! Now I see it's true that good things can be made even better through evil, and that when you ruin love and then rebuild it, it grows more beautiful than it was at first, as well as stronger and greater. So, having been rebuked for my mistake, I return to the person who makes me happy, and because of my evil deeds I get back three times what I spent.

120

That you were once unkind befriends me now,
And for that sorrow which I then did feel
Needs must I under my transgression bow,
Unless my nerves were brass or hammered steel.
For if you were by my unkindness shaken,
As I by yours, you've passed a hell of time,
And I, a tyrant, have no leisure taken
To weigh how once I suffered in your crime.
O that our night of woe might have rememb'red
My deepest sense, how hard true sorrow hits,
And soon to you as you to me then tendered
The humble salve which wounded bosoms fits!
  But that your trespass now becomes a fee;
  Mine ransoms yours, and yours must ransom me.

120

The fact that you were once cruel to me helps me now. Because of the sorrow that you made me feel then, I would have to be made of steel not to be bowed down to the ground with guilt over how I've hurt you. For if you've felt my unkindness to you the way I felt yours to me, you've endured a time in hell and I've acted like a cruel tyrant, never taking the time to think about how I once suffered when you committed the same crime against me. Oh, how I wish that your earlier sorrow had reminded me of how hard true sorrow hits, so that I would have apologized to you as fast as you apologized to me, giving you the medicine that an injured heart needs most! But your earlier offense against me can now compensate you for what I've just done. My offense cancels out yours, and yours must cancel out mine.

121

'Tis better to be vile than vile esteemed,
When not to be receives reproach of being,
And the just pleasure lost which is so deemed
Not by our feeling but by others' seeing.
For why should others' false adulterate eyes
Give salutation to my sportive blood?
Or on my frailties why are frailer spies,
Which in their wills count bad what I think good?
No, I am that I am, and they that level
At my abuses reckon up their own;
I may be straight, though they themselves be bevel.
By their rank thoughts my deeds must not be shown,
   Unless this general evil they maintain:
   All men are bad, and in their badness reign.

121

It's better to be vile than to have people think you're vile, especially when they accuse you of being vile and you're really not, and then you don't even get to enjoy doing the thing that people say is vile but that you don't think is. For why should people who are corrupt themselves get to wink knowingly at my lustful inclinations? And why should people who are even weaker than I pry into my weaknesses, deciding that what I think is good is bad? No, I am what I am, and the people who accuse me are only revealing their own corruptions. Maybe I'm straight, and they're the ones who are crooked; you can't measure my actions by their foul thoughts, unless they're willing to believe that all men are bad and thrive in their badness.

122

Thy gift, thy tables, are within my brain
Full charactered with lasting memory,
Which shall above that idle rank remain
Beyond all date, ev'n to eternity;
Or at the least, so long as brain and heart
Have faculty by nature to subsist;
Till each to razed oblivion yield his part
Of thee, thy record never can be missed.
That poor retention could not so much hold,
Nor need I tallies thy dear love to score;
Therefore to give them from me was I bold,
To trust those tables that receive thee more;
  To keep an adjunct to remember thee
  Were to import forgetfulness in me.

NO FEAR SHAKESPEARE

122

This sonnet can be read two ways: either the speaker was given a notebook in which the addressee had already written, or he was given a completely blank book. (This translation adopts the second reading.)

In my mind, I've already filled up the blank book you gave me with words that will remain in my memory longer than they would in that flimsy little book. In my memory, what I wrote about you will outlast any date, even to eternity. Or at least this record of you won't be lost as long as my brain and heart survive— until each of them is forced to give up its part of you and pass into oblivion. That poor little notebook couldn't hold as much as my memory can, and I have no need to keep notes to remember how much I love you. Therefore I was bold enough to give away your notebook, trusting in my own memory to keep a better record of you. For me to use an aid to remember you would imply that I'm forgetful.

123

No! Time, thou shalt not boast that I do change.
Thy pyramids built up with newer might
To me are nothing novel, nothing strange;
They are but dressings of a former sight.
Our dates are brief, and therefore we admire
What thou dost foist upon us that is old,
And rather make them born to our desire
Than think that we before have heard them told.
Thy registers and thee I both defy,
Not wond'ring at the present nor the past;
For thy recórds and what we see doth lie,
Made more or less by thy continual haste.
   This I do vow and this shall ever be:
   I will be true, despite thy scythe and thee.

NO FEAR SHAKESPEARE

123

No! Time, you're not going to boast that I change. These new enormous buildings that are being erected don't seem novel or strange to me at all—they're just replicas of what's existed before. Our lives are brief, and therefore we admire whatever is old, acting like it was made just for us rather than admitting we've heard it described before. I defy you and your records. I'm not interested in the present or the past, because both your records and the things we see around us lie. They are raised up and destroyed by your continual swift passage. I make this vow, and it shall always be true: I will be faithful despite you and your destructive power.

124

If my dear love were but the child of state,
It might for Fortune's bastard be unfathered,
As subject to time's love or to time's hate,
Weeds among weeds, or flow'rs with flowers gathered.
No, it was builded far from accident;
It suffers not in smiling pomp, nor falls
Under the blow of thrallèd discontent,
Whereto th' inviting time our fashion calls.
It fears not policy, that heretic,
Which works on leases of short numb'red hours.
But all alone stands hugely politic,
That it nor grows with heat nor drowns with showers.
   To this I witness call the fools of time,
    Which die for goodness, who have lived for crime.

124

If my great love for you had simply been created by circumstances, it might be rejected as illegitimate because changing circumstances could destroy it. It would be subject to whatever's in fashion at the moment, rejected with worthless things or plucked up with other fashionable flowers. No, my love was created where it can't be touched by the unpredictability of events. It's not helped by the approval of authority, nor is it crushed along with the malcontents who resist authority, as these times tempt us to do. My love isn't afraid of the political scheming and conniving engaged in by immoral people, which only has a short term effect, but stands by itself, independent and enormously wise, neither growing during times of pleasure nor killed by misfortune. To attest to what I'm saying, I call as witnesses all those fools who died repentant and seeking goodness after living lives dedicated to crime.

125

Were't ought to me I bore the canopy,
With my extern the outward honoring,
Or laid great bases for eternity,
Which prove more short than waste or ruining?
Have I not seen dwellers on form and favor
Lose all and more by paying too much rent,
For compound sweet forgoing simple savor,
Pitiful thrivers, in their gazing spent?
No, let me be obsequious in thy heart,
And take thou my oblation, poor but free,
Which is not mixed with seconds, knows no art,
But mutual render, only me for thee.
   Hence, thou suborned informer! A true soul
   When most impeached stands least in thy control.

NO FEAR SHAKESPEARE

125

Would it matter at all to me to carry the ceremonial canopy of a monarch in a procession, honoring the display of power with my appearance? Or would I think it worthwhile to lay the foundations of supposedly eternal monuments, which actually last only as long as decay or ruin permit? Haven't I seen those who focus on appearances and covet the favors of the powerful lose everything, and more than everything, by spending too much on their obsessions? Such pitiful strivers give up simple pleasures for the sake of lavish meals, using up all their resources on their fickle desires. No, I shall be obedient and faithful to you only, and you shall accept my offering. It is simple but freely given, contains nothing second-rate, no unnecessary additions, only mutual surrender: myself for yourself. Get out of here, you paid spy: When a faithful person like I am is accused, someone like you has no power over them.

The "suborned informer" (paid spy) whom the speaker addresses in the last sentence is mysterious. Editors are unsure whom this figure is supposed to represent.

126

O thou, my lovely boy, who in thy pow'r
Dost hold time's fickle glass, his sickle hour,
Who hast by waning grown, and therein show'st
Thy lovers withering, as thy sweet self grow'st—
If nature, sovereign mistress over wrack,
As thou goest onwards still will pluck thee back,
She keeps thee to this purpose: that her skill
May time disgrace, and wretched minute kill.
Yet fear her, O thou minion of her pleasure;
She may detain, but not still keep, her treasure.
Her audit, though delayed, answered must be,
And her quietus is to render thee.
(   )
(   )

126

Oh, my lovely boy, you seem to have power over time itself, immune to its capacity to cut things down. You've only grown more beautiful as you've aged, revealing in the process how withered I, your lover, have become. If nature, which has power over destruction, has chosen to hold you back from decay, she's doing so for this reason: to disgrace time and kill its effects. Yet in spite of this, you should fear her, though you're nature's best-loved pet. She can preserve you for a time, but she can't keep you, her treasure, always. Nature will eventually be called to offer her accounts, and though she can delay this, she has to do it, and the way she'll pay her debt to time is with you. (   )
(   )

The parentheses appear in the original printed edition of the Sonnets, perhaps indicating silence where we would expect the final couplet.

127

In the old age black was not counted fair,
Or if it were, it bore not beauty's name.
But now is black beauty's successive heir,
And beauty slandered with a bastard shame.
For since each hand hath put on nature's pow'r,
Fairing the foul with art's false borrowed face,
Sweet beauty hath no name, no holy bow'r,
But is profaned, if not lives in disgrace.
Therefore my mistress' eyes are raven black,
Her eyes so suited, and they mourners seem
At such who, not born fair, no beauty lack,
Sland'ring creation with a false esteem.
  Yet so they mourn, becoming of their woe,
  That every tongue says beauty should look so.

127

In the olden days, dark complexions weren't considered attractive or, if they were, no one called them beautiful. But now darkness is officially accepted as beautiful, and the fair complexions that used to be called beautiful have gotten a bad reputation. For since everyone has seized the power to make themselves beautiful (which used to belong to nature), and ugly people can be beautiful by artificial means, no one can legitimately be called beautiful. Beauty has no special home but is commonplace or even lives in disgrace. Therefore my mistress's eyes are as black as a raven, well suited to today's fashion, and in their blackness they seem to be lamenting those people who were born ugly but make themselves beautiful, giving beauty a bad name by faking it. But her black eyes lament so beautifully that everyone now says all beautiful eyes should look like hers.

128

How oft when thou, my music, music play'st
Upon that blessèd wood whose motion sounds
With thy sweet fingers, when thou gently sway'st
The wiry concord that mine ear confounds,
Do I envy´ those jacks that nimble leap
To kiss the tender inward of thy hand,
Whilst my poor lips, which should that harvest reap,
At the wood's boldness by thee blushing stand.
To be so tickled they would change their state
And situation with those dancing chips,
O'er whom thy fingers walk with gentle gait,
Making dead wood more blest than living lips.
   Since saucy jacks so happy are in this,
    Give them thy fingers, me thy lips to kiss.

NO FEAR SHAKESPEARE

128

Very often, when you (my greatest source of delight) play music by moving those wooden keys on the keyboard of the virginal with your sweet fingers, confusing my ear with the harmony of those plucked strings, I envy the keys. They leap up and kiss the tender underside of your hands, while my poor lips, who ought to be doing the kissing, stand by, blushing at the boldness of the keys. To be tickled like those keys are, my lips would gladly be transformed into wood and change places with the keys, over which your fingers gently walk, blessing the dead wood more than my living lips. Since the keys are so happy to touch your fingers, let them have the fingers, but give me your lips to kiss.

The virginal is a keyboard instrument similar to a harpsichord.

129

Th' expense of spirit in a waste of shame
Is lust in action, and till action, lust
Is perjured, murd'rous, bloody, full of blame,
Savage, extreme, rude, cruel, not to trust,
Enjoyed no sooner but despisèd straight,
Past reason hunted, and no sooner had,
Past reason hated as a swallowed bait
On purpose laid to make the taker mad;
Mad in pursuit, and in possession so,
Had, having, and in quest to have, extreme;
A bliss in proof, and proved, a very woe;
Before, a joy proposed; behind, a dream.
    All this the world well knows, yet none knows well
    To shun the heaven that leads men to this hell.

129

Sex is a way of squandering vital energy while incurring shame. In anticipation of sex, lust makes people murderous, violent, blameworthy, savage, extreme, rude, cruel, and untrustworthy. No sooner do people enjoy sex than they immediately despise it. They go to absurd lengths in its pursuit only to hate it out of all proportion once they've had it, insisting it was put in their path on purpose to make them crazy. They're extreme when they're pursuing sex, extreme when they're having it, and extreme once they've had it. It's blissful while you're doing it and, once you're done, a true sorrow. While you're anticipating it, it seems like a joy; afterward, like a bad dream. The world knows all this very well, yet no one knows enough to avoid the heavenly experience that leads us to this hell.

130

My mistress' eyes are nothing like the sun;
Coral is far more red than her lips' red;
If snow be white, why then her breasts are dun;
If hairs be wires, black wires grow on her head;
I have seen roses damasked, red and white,
But no such roses see I in her cheeks;
And in some pérfumes is there more delight
Than in the breath that from my mistress reeks.
I love to hear her speak, yet well I know
That music hath a far more pleasing sound.
I grant I never saw a goddess go;
My mistress, when she walks, treads on the ground.
   And yet, by heaven, I think my love as rare
   As any she belied with false compare.

NO FEAR SHAKESPEARE

130

My mistress's eyes are nothing like the sun. Coral is much redder than the red of her lips. Compared to the whiteness of snow, her breasts are grayish-brown. Poets describe their mistresses' hair as gold wires, but my mistress has *black* wires growing on her head. I have seen roses that were a mixture of red and white, but I don't see those colors in her cheeks. And some perfumes smell more delightful than my mistress's reeking breath. I love to hear her speak; yet I know perfectly well that music has a far more pleasant sound. I admit I never saw a goddess walk; when my mistress walks, she treads on the ground. And yet, by heaven, I think my beloved is as special as any woman whom poets have lied about with false comparisons.

131

Thou art as tyrannous, so as thou art,
As those whose beauties proudly make them cruel;
For well thou know'st, to my dear doting heart
Thou art the fairest and most precious jewel.
Yet in good faith some say, that thee behold,
Thy face hath not the pow'r to make love groan.
To say they err I dare not be so bold,
Although I swear it to myself alone;
And to be sure that is not false, I swear
A thousand groans but thinking on thy face;
One on another's neck do witness bear
Thy black is fairest in my judgment's place.
   In nothing art thou black save in thy deeds,
   And thence this slander, as I think, proceeds.

131

Even looking like you do, you're as much of a tyrant as those women whose beauty makes them proud and cruel. For you know quite well that to me, who dotes on you, you're the most beautiful and precious jewel. Yet some people say, in all honesty after looking at you, that your face simply does not have what it takes to make someone groan with love. I wouldn't dare be so bold as to tell them they're wrong, though to myself I swear they are. And to prove to myself that I'm right, I groan a thousand times just thinking about your face. These groans, coming one after the other, testify to the fact that your dark complexion is the most beautiful one to my eyes. There's nothing black about you except your actions, and I think that's the reason people spread this lie about your looks.

132

Thine eyes I love, and they, as pitying me,
Knowing thy heart torment me with disdain,
Have put on black, and loving mourners be,
Looking with pretty ruth upon my pain;
And truly, not the morning sun of heav'n
Better becomes the gray cheeks of the east,
Nor that full star that ushers in the ev'n
Doth half that glory to the sober west,
As those two mourning eyes become thy face.
O let it then as well beseem thy heart
To mourn for me, since mourning doth thee grace,
And suit thy pity like in every part.
   Then will I swear beauty herself is black,
   And all they foul that thy complexion lack.

132

I love your eyes, and they seem to pity me, knowing I'm tormented by your disdain. In black, they look like mourners at a funeral, gazing at my pain with pretty compassion. And to tell the truth, the morning sun doesn't look as good in the gray eastern sky, nor does the evening star look half as good in the western twilight, as those two mourning eyes look in your face. Oh, then I hope it would be just as beautiful for your heart to pity me, too, since mourning suits you so well, and for you to pity me with every other part of you to match. If you take pity on me, I'll swear beauty itself is black, and everyone who doesn't have your dark complexion is ugly.

133

Beshrew that heart that makes my heart to groan
For that deep wound it gives my friend and me;
Is't not enough to torture me alone,
But slave to slavery my sweet'st friend must be?
Me from myself thy cruel eye hath taken,
And my next self thou harder hast engrossed;
Of him, myself, and thee I am forsaken,
A torment thrice threefold thus to be crossed.
Prison my heart in thy steel bosom's ward,
But then my friend's heart let my poor heart bail.
Whoe'er keeps me, let my heart be his guard;
Thou canst not then use rigor in my jail.
  And yet thou wilt, for I being pent in thee,
  Perforce am thine, and all that is in me.

133

Curse you for making me suffer by hurting both my friend and me. Isn't it enough to torture me alone without making my friend your slave too? Because of your cruel attractions I'm no longer my own man, but my friend, who's like my second self, you've enslaved even more cruelly. So I've been abandoned by him, by myself, and by you; being frustrated like this is a triple torment multiplied by three. Go ahead and keep me as your prisoner, but then let me use myself to bail out my friend. Whoever you assign to watch me while I'm in this jail, let me be in charge of guarding my friend— then you can't torment me in my prison because I'll have my friend to keep me happy. And yet you *will* torment me, because I belong to you, so everything that's in me is yours, and since my friend is in my heart, he's yours too.

134

So now I have confessed that he is thine,
And I myself am mortgaged to thy will,
Myself I'll forfeit, so that other mine
Thou wilt restore to be my comfort still.
But thou wilt not, nor he will not be free,
For thou art covetous, and he is kind.
He learned but surety-like to write for me,
Under that bond that him as fast doth bind.
The statute of thy beauty thou wilt take,
Thou usurer, that put'st forth all to use,
And sue a friend came debtor for my sake;
So him I lose through my unkind abuse.
   Him have I lost; thou hast both him and me;
   He pays the whole, and yet am I not free.

134

(Continuing from Sonnet 133) So now I've admitted that he's yours, and I'm legally bound to satisfy your desires too. I'll give myself up to you if you'll let go of my friend, so he can come back and comfort me. But you won't let him go, and he doesn't want to be free, because you're greedy and he's kind. He only became your slave because he was trying to bail me out, like someone co-signing a loan, but now he's just as much under your power as I am. You're going to insist on taking what your beauty entitles you to, you loan shark—you loan your body to everybody, and then you go after my friend, who only took you up on it for my sake. So I lose my friend because I allowed him to get tangled up with you. I've lost him; you have both him and me; he's giving you all the sex you're owed, but I'm still not free.

135

Whoever hath her wish, thou hast thy Will,
And Will to boot, and Will in overplus;
More than enough am I, that vex thee still,
To thy sweet will making addition thus.
Wilt thou, whose will is large and spacious,
Not once vouchsafe to hide my will in thine?
Shall will in others seem right gracious,
And in my will no fair acceptance shine?
The sea, all water, yet receives rain still,
And in abundance addeth to his store;
So thou, being rich in Will, add to thy Will
One will of mine, to make thy large Will more.
   Let no unkind, no fair beseechers kill;
    Think all but one, and me in that one Will.

135

Other women may have their little desires, but you have your Will, and another Will as well, and more Will than you need. I, who am constantly pestering you for sex, am more than enough to satisfy you, adding another willing penis to the Will you already have. Since your sexual desires (and vagina) are both so enormous, won't you agree just once to let me put my desire inside yours? Are you going to be attracted to everyone else's will (penis), but reject mine? The sea is entirely made of water, but it still accepts additional water whenever it rains. So you, who already have a William, should in addition to your lover William accept my will (penis), making your sexual appetite (or vagina), which is already huge, even huger. Don't kill an eager seducer by being unkind to him. Treat all your lovers as a single lover, and accept me (and my part) as part of that lover.

The speaker is named Will, but the woman he's addressing has another lover who is also named Will. In this sonnet, the word *will* is used thirteen times, meaning "William," "sexual desire," "penis," or "vagina," depending on the context (and it usually means more than one of these things at once).

136

If thy soul check thee that I come so near,
Swear to thy blind soul that I was thy Will,
And will, thy soul knows, is admitted there;
Thus far for love my love-suit sweet fulfill.
Will will fulfill the treasure of thy love,
Ay, fill it full with wills, and my will one.
In things of great receipt with ease we prove
Among a number one is reckoned none.
Then in the number let me pass untold,
Though in thy store's account I one must be.
For nothing hold me, so it please thee hold
That nothing me, a something sweet to thee.
　　Make but my name thy love, and love that still;
　　And then thou lov'st me, for my name is Will.

136

(Continuing from Sonnet 135) If it's bothering your blind conscience that I keep pressing you for sex, just tell it that I'm Will, your lover—your conscience knows that Will is allowed in your bed. Out of charity, give in to my request at least that much. Will will fill your sweet love-treasure until it's full. Yes, he'll fill it full of penises, and mine will be one of them. With things that can hold a lot (like your vagina), it's clear that one of anything is never enough. So among your vast number of lovers, let me be included without counting me. Consider me to be nothing, as long as you consider the nothing that I am to be sweet to you. Just love my name and love it always, and then you'll love me, because my name is Will.

As in 135, Will the speaker address-es a woman who has another lover named Will and puns on the word will *in the sense of "William," "penis," and "sexual desire."*

137

Thou blind fool love, what dost thou to mine eyes,
That they behold, and see not what they see?
They know what beauty is, see where it lies,
Yet what the best is take the worst to be.
If eyes corrupt by over-partial looks
Be anchored in the bay where all men ride,
Why of eyes' falsehood hast thou forgèd hooks,
Whereto the judgment of my heart is tied?
Why should my heart think that a several plot
Which my heart knows the wide world's common place?
Or mine eyes, seeing this, say this is not,
To put fair truth upon so foul a face?
   In things right true my heart and eyes have erred,
   And to this false plague are they now transferred.

137

Love, you blind fool, what are you doing to my eyes that's keeping them from accurately seeing what I look at? My eyes know what beauty is, and they see who has it, yet they decide that the worst woman is the best. Love, if my vision has been distorted because I look at her with too much bias, spending all my time staring at this woman who sleeps with every man, why have you used my misperceptions as a trap to fool my heart, so that I love the wrong person? Why should my heart think that she could belong to one man when my heart knows she's available to the whole world? Or why should my eyes witness her promiscuity but act like it's not true, putting a good face on an ugly truth? My heart and my eyes have been completely mistaken about the truth, and now they both love this unfaithful disease of a woman.

138

When my love swears that she is made of truth
I do believe her, though I know she lies,
That she might think me some untutored youth
Unlearnèd in the world's false subtleties.
Thus vainly thinking that she thinks me young,
Although she knows my days are past the best,
Simply I credit her false speaking tongue;
On both sides thus is simple truth suppressed.
But wherefore says she not she is unjust?
And wherefore say not I that I am old?
O love's best habit is in seeming trust,
And age in love loves not t' have years told.
   Therefore I lie with her, and she with me,
   And in our faults by lies we flattered be.

138

When my mistress swears that she's completely truthful, I believe her even though I know she lies, so that she'll think that I'm some naïve young man who's ignorant about the world and the tricks people play. I pretend to stupidly believe her lies while fooling myself into thinking that she thinks I'm young, even though she knows I'm past my prime. In this way, both of us suppress the simple truth. But why doesn't she say she's a liar? And why don't I say that I'm old? Oh, because it's easiest to love someone who seems to be trustworthy, and old people who are in love hate to hear their age discussed. Therefore, I sleep with her, and she sleeps with me, and we both flatter ourselves by lying about each other's faults.

139

O call not me to justify the wrong
That thy unkindness lays upon my heart.
Wound me not with thine eye, but with thy tongue;
Use pow'r with pow'r, and slay me not by art.
Tell me thou lov'st elsewhére; but in my sight,
Dear heart, forbear to glance thine eye aside.
What need'st thou wound with cunning when thy might
Is more than my o'er-pressed defense can bide?
Let me excuse thee: Ah, my love well knows
Her pretty looks have been mine enemies,
And therefore from my face she turns my foes,
That they elsewhére might dart their injuries.
    Yet do not so, but since I am near slain,
    Kill me outríght with looks, and rid my pain.

139

Oh, don't ask me to justify the cruel infidelities with which you have hurt me. Don't hurt me by stealing glances at other men; hurt me by telling me about them to my face. Use your power openly, don't kill me with subtle tricks. Tell me you love other people, but when you're in my sight, dear heart, don't glance at other men. Why would you need to hurt me with cunning, when your power over me is already too much for me to defend against? But I'll make an excuse for you: Ah, my love knows perfectly well that her looks can kill me, so she looks away from me to kill my enemies instead. But don't do that. Since I'm almost dead already, kill me outright with your looks, and put me out of my misery.

140

Be wise as thou art cruel; do not press
My tongue-tied patience with too much disdain,
Lest sorrow lend me words, and words express
The manner of my pity-wanting pain.
If I might teach thee wit, better it were,
Though not to love, yet love, to tell me so,
As testy sick men, when their deaths be near,
No news but health from their physicians know.
For if I should despair, I should grow mad,
And in my madness might speak ill of thee.
Now this ill-wresting world is grown so bad,
Mad sland'rers by mad ears believèd be.
    That I may not be so, nor thou belied,
    Bear thine eyes straight, though thy proud heart go wide.

NO FEAR SHAKESPEARE

140

Be as wise as you are cruel: Don't torture me too much with your disdain, in case sorrow forces me to speak, and I express how pitiless you are in hurting me. If you'll let me teach you some skill—it would be better if you told me you loved me even if you don't, as when short-tempered patients close to death get only good news from their doctors. Because if I start to despair, I'll go mad, and in my madness I might speak ill of you. This world has gotten so bad with its lies and rumors that crazy people believe the lies that crazy people tell. To prevent my going crazy and your being lied about, keep your eyes where they should be, even when your heart's wandering where it wants.

141

In faith, I do not love thee with mine eyes,
For they in thee a thousand errors note;
But 'tis my heart that loves what they despise,
Who in despite of view is pleased to dote.
Nor are mine ears with thy tongue's tune delighted,
Nor tender feeling to base touches prone,
Nor taste, nor smell, desire to be invited
To any sensual feast with thee alone.
But my five wits, nor my five senses, can
Dissuade one foolish heart from serving thee,
Who leaves unswayed the likeness of a man,
Thy proud heart's slave and vassal wretch to be.
   Only my plague thus far I count my gain,
   That she that makes me sin awards me pain.

141

I swear, I don't love you with my eyes: They notice a thousand flaws in you. Rather, it's my heart that loves what my eyes despise; despite what you look like, my heart dotes on you. Nor are my ears delighted by the sound of your voice. Nor do I want to abuse my delicate sense of touch by groping you. Nor do my sense of taste or smell want to be invited to any feast of the senses in which you're the main course. But neither my brain nor my five senses can dissuade my foolish heart from being your servant. My body stands here like an empty shell with no one to control it, while my heart goes off to be your slave and wretched property. I gain one thing from being plagued with love for this woman: The same woman who's making me sin rewards me with pain.

142

Love is my sin, and thy dear virtue hate,
Hate of my sin, grounded on sinful loving.
O but with mine compare thou thine own state,
And thou shalt find it merits not reproving;
Or, if it do, not from those lips of thine,
That have profaned their scarlet ornaments
And sealed false bonds of love as oft as mine,
Robbed others' beds' revénues of their rents.
Be it lawful I love thee as thou lov'st those
Whom thine eyes woo as mine impórtune thee.
Root pity in thy heart, that when it grows,
Thy pity may deserve to pitied be.
   If thou dost seek to have what thou dost hide,
   By self-example mayst thou be denied.

NO FEAR SHAKESPEARE

142

Loving you is my sin, and your precious virtue consists in hating my sin, a hate grounded in your own sinful loving. But compare my moral state with your own, and you'll see I don't deserve to be reprimanded, or if I do, not from those lips of yours, which you've dishonored by using too much. Your lips have kissed as many people and made as many false promises as mine have, and both of us have cheated on our partners, giving away sexual favors where they don't belong. If I may be allowed to love you the same way you love those other men whom you seduce with your glances, have a little pity for me; then you'll deserve to be pitied yourself. If you want people to take pity on you and sleep with you, but you don't show pity for me, you might be turned down because of your own example.

143

Lo, as a careful housewife runs to catch
One of her feathered creatures broke away,
Sets down her babe and makes all swift dispatch
In pursuit of the thing she would have stay;
Whilst her neglected child holds her in chase,
Cries to catch her whose busy care is bent
To follow that which flies before her face,
Not prizing her poor infant's discontent:
So run'st thou after that which flies from thee,
Whilst I, thy babe, chase thee afar behind.
But if thou catch thy hope, turn back to me,
And play the mother's part, kiss me, be kind.
  So will I pray that thou mayst have thy Will,
  If thou turn back and my loud crying still.

143

Like an anxious housewife who runs to catch one of her chickens that's run away, setting down her baby to follow it while her neglected child chases after her and cries out to get her attention—she focusing all of her mind on trying to catch the chicken that's flying in front of her, not caring about her infant's distress—in the same way, you're running after someone who's running from you, while I, your baby, chase after you from far behind. But if you catch the one you're hoping for, turn back to me and act like a mother. Kiss me, be kind. If you'll turn back and stop my loud crying, I'll pray that you'll get to have your Will.

As in Sonnets 135 and 136, the speaker's mistress loves a man named Will who is not the speaker.

144

Two loves I have, of comfort and despair,
Which, like two spirits, do suggest me still;
The better angel is a man right fair,
The worser spirit a woman colored ill.
To win me soon to hell, my female evil
Tempteth my better angel from my side,
And would corrupt my saint to be a devil,
Wooing his purity with her foul pride.
And whether that my angel be turned fiend
Suspect I may, but not directly tell;
But being both from me both to each friend,
I guess one angel in another's hell.
 Yet this shall I ne'er know, but live in doubt,
 Till my bad angel fire my good one out.

144

I love two people. One comforts me and the other makes me despair. Like two spirits both constantly point me in different directions. The better angel is a beautiful, fair-haired man. The bad one is an evil-looking woman. To help put me in hell sooner, my evil female tempts my angel away from my side. She hopes to make my saint into a devil, seducing him to impure acts in her foul and self-assured way. And though I can suspect him, there's no way I can tell directly whether my angel has turned into a fiend. But since the two of them are away from me and friendly with each other, I'm guessing that one angel is inside the other—and in hell with her. Yet I'll never know this for sure, instead living in doubt until my bad angel fires the good one out of hell.

The bad angel's "fire" suggests the burning sensations of venereal disease.

145

Those lips that love's own hand did make
Breathed forth the sound that said "I hate"
To me that languished for her sake;
But when she saw my woeful state,
Straight in her heart did mercy come,
Chiding that tongue that, ever sweet,
Was used in giving gentle doom,
And taught it thus anew to greet:
"I hate" she altered with an end
That followed it as gentle day
Doth follow night, who like a fiend
From heav'n to hell is flown away.
　　"I hate" from hate away she threw,
　　And saved my life, saying "not you."

NO FEAR SHAKESPEARE

145

Those lips that look like they were made by the goddess of love herself breathed forth the words, "I hate"—and she was talking to me, the man who's pining with love for her. But when she saw how unhappy she'd made me, mercy came into her heart and she chided her sweet tongue, which is usually so gentle and merciful, and taught it to speak something else to me. She changed "I hate" by adding a few words the way day follows night, that fiend flying from heaven to hell: She took hatred away from "I hate," saving my life with "not you."

146

Poor soul, the center of my sinful earth,

[Thrall to] these rebel pow'rs that thee array,

Why dost thou pine within and suffer dearth,

Painting thy outward walls so costly gay?

Why so large cost, having so short a lease,

Dost thou upon thy fading mansion spend?

Shall worms, inheritors of this excess,

Eat up thy charge? Is this thy body's end?

Then, soul, live thou upon thy servant's loss,

And let that pine to aggravate thy store;

Buy terms divine in selling hours of dross;

Within be fed, without be rich no more.

   So shalt thou feed on death, that feeds on men,

    And death once dead, there's no more dying then.

Due to a printer's error in the earliest edition of the Sonnets, no one knows what Shakespeare intended for the first two syllables of line 2. The guesses editors have made over the centuries include "Thrall to," "Hemm'd by," "Fool'd by," "Foil'd by," and "Feeding."

146

My poor soul, you're the very center of this sinful world, my body, which rebels against you. Why do you starve yourself inside me and suffer from a shortage of supplies while you dress your outside in such expensive finery? Why do you spend so much on your aging body when you get to occupy it for such a short time? All of this expenditure on a body that is eventually going to be eaten by the worms—do you want what you spend to be devoured by worms? Is this what your body was intended for? In that case, soul, feed yourself by starving your body; let *it* pine for food while *you* accumulate the riches. Buy time in heaven by giving up worthless time wasted on earth. Feed your inner self; let your body be poor. By starving your body, you will eat up death, which eats up men, and once death is dead, there's no more dying then.

147

My love is as a fever, longing still
For that which longer nurseth the disease,
Feeding on that which doth preserve the ill,
Th' uncertain sickly appetite to please.
My reason, the physician to my love,
Angry that his prescriptions are not kept,
Hath left me, and I desp'rate now approve
Desire is death, which physic did except.
Past cure I am, now reason is past care,
And frantic mad with evermore unrest,
My thoughts and my discourse as madmen's are,
At random from the truth vainly expressed;
    For I have sworn thee fair and thought thee bright,
    Who art as black as hell, as dark as night.

NO FEAR SHAKESPEARE

147

My love is like a fever, always making me yearn for what will prolong my disease. It lives on whatever will preserve the illness, in order to prop up my fickle desire. My reasoning has acted as doctor and treated my love, but then it left me because I wasn't following its instructions. Now that I'm finally desperate enough, I realize that sexual desire, which was against the doctor's orders, is lethal. Now that my mind is past caring, I'm past the point where I can be cured, and I've gone frantically crazy and grown increasingly restless. My thoughts and speech are like a madman's, pointlessly expressing random untruths. For I have sworn that you're beautiful and thought you radiant when you're actually as black as hell and as dark as night.

148

O me! what eyes hath love put in my head,
Which have no correspondence with true sight!
Or, if they have, where is my judgment fled,
That censures falsely what they see aright?
If that be fair whereon my false eyes dote,
What means the world to say it is not so?
If it be not, then love doth well denote
Love's eye is not so true as all men's: no,
How can it? O how can love's eye be true,
That is so vexed with watching and with tears?
No marvel then, though I mistake my view;
The sun itself sees not till heaven clears.
   O cunning love! With tears thou keep'st me blind,
   Lest eyes well seeing thy foul faults should find.

148

Oh, me! What kind of eyes has love put into my head that I don't see anything accurately? Or if my eyes do see correctly, what's happened to my judgment to make me wrongly criticize what they see? If the woman I love to look at is beautiful, why does the rest of the world say she's not? If she's not, then a person in love doesn't see as accurately as others. No—how can a lover see right? Oh, how can a lover's eye work properly when it's so distressed by staying awake and crying? It's no wonder then that I'm wrong about what I see; the sun itself doesn't see anything until the sky is clear. Oh, ingenious love, you keep me blind with tears so I won't discover my lover's foul faults, as I would if my eyes worked properly.

149

Canst thou, O cruel, say I love thee not,
When I against myself with thee partake?
Do I not think on thee, when I forgot
Am of myself, all, tyrant, for thy sake?
Who hateth thee that I do call my friend?
On whom frown'st thou that I do fawn upon?
Nay, if thou lour'st on me, do I not spend
Revenge upon myself with present moan?
What merit do I in myself respect,
That is so proud thy service to despise,
When all my best doth worship thy defect,
Commanded by the motion of thine eyes?
  But, love, hate on, for now I know thy mind;
  Those that can see thou lov'st, and I am blind.

149

Oh, you cruel woman, can you say I don't love you when I take sides with you against myself? Don't I think about you even when I've forgotten about myself—and all for your sake, you tyrant? Who hates you that I would call my friend? Who do you frown at that I grovel on and flatter? No—if you scowl at me, don't I immediately punish myself by moaning? Which quality do I see in myself that would make me too proud to be your servant? All of the best in me worships the worst in you, and you can command me with a glance. But, my love, go on hating me, because now I know your mind. You love people who can see, and I'm blind.

150

O from what pow'r hast thou this pow'rful might,
With insufficiency my heart to sway,
To make me give the lie to my true sight,
And swear that brightness doth not grace the day?
Whence hast thou this becoming of things ill,
That in the very refuse of thy deeds
There is such strength and warrantise of skill
That in my mind thy worst all best exceeds?
Who taught thee how to make me love thee more,
The more I hear and see just cause of hate?
O, though I love what others do abhor,
With others thou shouldst not abhor my state.
   If thy unworthiness raised love in me,
   More worthy I to be beloved of thee.

NO FEAR SHAKESPEARE

150

Oh, what is the source of this mighty power you have, which controls my affections despite your inadequacies, making me disbelieve what my eyes truly see until I'm so turned around I swear that daylight isn't bright? Where did you get this capacity to make bad things look good in you, to perform the most worthless actions so skillfully that I think your worst is better than anyone else's best? Who taught you how to make me love you more, the more I hear and see good reasons to hate you? Oh, even though I love what other people despise, you shouldn't despise my love the way other people do. Since your unworthiness made me love you, I'm the person who deserves your love.

151

Love is too young to know what conscience is,
Yet who knows not conscience is born of love?
Then, gentle cheater, urge not my amiss,
Lest guilty of my faults thy sweet self prove;
For, thou betraying me, I do betray
My nobler part to my gross body's treason.
My soul doth tell my body that he may
Triumph in love—flesh stays no father reason,
But, rising at thy name, doth point out thee
As his triumphant prize—proud of this pride,
He is contented thy poor drudge to be,
To stand in thy affairs, fall by thy side.
  No want of conscience hold it that I call
  Her "love" for whose dear love I rise and fall.

NO FEAR SHAKESPEARE

151

Cupid is too young to know right from wrong, but doesn't everybody know that love is what gives you a conscience? In that case, gentle cheater, don't criticize me too harshly for my mistake, because your sweet self might turn out to be guilty of the same faults. Because you betray me, I betray my soul to my dumb, rebellious body. My soul tells my body that it can have its way in love. My flesh doesn't wait to hear any more, but at the sound of your name it rises up and points you out as its prize. My flesh, proud of having you, is happy to be your poor worker, to stand up to do your business and fall down beside you afterward. Do not assume my conscience is lacking just because the woman I call "love" makes my flesh rise and fall for her love.

152

In loving thee thou know'st I am forsworn;
But thou art twice forsworn to me love swearing,
In act thy bed-vow broke and new faith torn,
In vowing new hate after new love bearing.
But why of two oaths' breach do I accuse thee,
When I break twenty? I am perjured most,
For all my vows are oaths but to misuse thee,
And all my honest faith in thee is lost;
For I have sworn deep oaths of thy deep kindness,
Oaths of thy love, thy truth, thy constancy,
And, to enlighten thee, gave eyes to blindness,
Or made them swear against the thing they see.
　For I have sworn thee fair: more perjured eye,
　To swear against the truth so foul a lie.

152

I know I'm breaking a promise by loving you, but you, swearing you love me, are breaking two promises: cheating on your husband by leaving his bed, then breaking your promise to your new lover by vowing to hate him. But why am I accusing you of breaking two oaths when I break twenty? I am perjured the most, because all of my vows are only made to mislead and exploit you; I'm no longer true to you. For I have sworn great oaths about how kind you are, oaths about your love, your faithfulness, your constancy. And to make you look better I blinded myself, swearing to the opposite of what I actually saw. For I have sworn that you are beautiful; my eye is doubly a liar, offering such a foul lie after swearing to tell the truth.

153

Cupid laid by his brand and fell asleep.
A maid of Dian's this advantage found,
And his love-kindling fire did quickly steep
In a cold valley-fountain of that ground,
Which borrowed from this holy fire of love
A dateless lively heat, still to endure,
And grew a seething bath, which yet men prove
Against strange maladies a sovereign cure.
But at my mistress' eye love's brand new fired,
The boy for trial needs would touch my breast;
I, sick withal, the help of bath desired,
And thither hied, a sad distempered guest,
   But found no cure; the bath for my help lies
   Where Cupid got new fire—my mistress' eye.

153

Sonnets 153 and 154 are full of double entendres of sexual intercourse followed by venereal disease.

Diana is the goddess of chastity and virginity, so the nymphs devoted to her are opposed to Cupid and erotic love, represented by his torch.

Cupid put down his torch and fell asleep. One of the nymphs who serve Diana took advantage of this situation and quickly plunged Cupid's love-inducing flame in a nearby cold spring, which thus acquired a never-ending heat and became a bubbling hot bath that men still use to cure diseases. But at a glance from my mistress, Cupid's torch fired up again, and Cupid decided to test whether his torch was working by touching my heart with it. I became sick with love and wanted the bath to ease my discomfort. I went to the spring as a sad, sick guest but found no cure. The only thing that could help me is the thing that gave Cupid his new fire: a glance from my mistress's eye.

154

The little love-god lying once asleep
Laid by his side his heart-inflaming brand,
Whilst many nymphs that vowed chaste life to keep
Came tripping by; but in her maiden hand
The fairest votary took up that fire,
Which many legions of true hearts had warmed;
And so the general of hot desire
Was, sleeping, by a virgin hand disarmed.
This brand she quenchèd in a cool well by,
Which from love's fire took heat perpetual,
Growing a bath and healthful remedy
For men diseased; but I, my mistress' thrall,
   Came there for cure, and this by that I prove:
   Love's fire heats water; water cools not love.

FINIS.

154

Once, while sleeping, little Cupid put down his love-inducing torch while many of Diana's nymphs, who had all made lifelong vows of chastity, came tripping by. But the most beautiful of Diana's nymphs picked up that fire that had warmed the hearts of legions of faithful lovers. In this fashion, the commander of hot desire was disarmed by the hand of a virgin as he was sleeping. She quenched this torch in a cool spring nearby, and the spring took a perpetual heat from love's fire. It turned into a hot bath and healthy remedy for diseased men. But when I, enslaved by my mistress, went to the bath to be cured, this is what I learned: Love's fire heats water, but water doesn't cool love.

THE END

Index of First Lines

How oft when thou, my music, music play'st 256
How sweet and lovely dost thou make the shame 190
I grant thou wert not married to my muse, 164
I never saw that you did painting need, 166
If my dear love were but the child of state, 248
If the dull substance of my flesh were thought, 88
If there be nothing new, but that which is 118
If thou survive my well-contented day, 64
If thy soul check thee that I come so near, 272
In faith, I do not love thee with mine eyes, 282
In loving thee thou know'st I am forsworn; 304
In the old age black was not counted fair, 254
Is it for fear to wet a widow's eye 18
Is it thy will thy image should keep open 122
Let me confess that we two must be twain, 72
Let me not to the marriage of true minds 232
Let not my love be called idolatry, 210
Let those who are in favor with their stars 50
Like as the waves make towards the pebbled shore, 120
Like as to make our appetites more keen 236
Lo, as a careful housewife runs to catch 286
Lo, in the Orient when the gracious light 14
Look in thy glass and tell the face thou viewest, 6
Lord of my love, to whom in vassalage 52
Love is my sin, and thy dear virtue hate, 284
Love is too young to know what conscience is, 302
Mine eye and heart are at a mortal war 92
Mine eye hath played the painter and hath steeled 48
Music to hear, why hear'st thou music sadly? 16
My glass shall not persuade me I am old 44
My love is as a fever, longing still 294
My love is strengthened, though more weak in seeming; 204
My mistress' eyes are nothing like the sun; 260
My tongue-tied muse in manners holds her still, 170
No longer mourn for me when I am dead 142
No more be grieved at that which thou hast done. 70

No! Time, thou shalt not boast that I do change. 246
Not from the stars do I my judgment pluck, 28
Not marble nor the gilded monuments 110
Not mine own fears, nor the prophetic soul 214
O call not me to justify the wrong 278
O for my sake do you with Fortune chide, 222
O from what pow'r hast thou this pow'rful might, 300
O how I faint when I of you do write, 160
O how much more doth beauty beauteous seem 108
O how thy worth with manners may I sing, 78
O lest the world should task you to recite 144
O me! what eyes hath love put in my head, 296
O never say that I was false of heart, 218
O that you were yourself! But, love, you are 26
O thou, my lovely boy, who in thy pow'r 252
O truant Muse, what shall be thy amends 202
Or I shall live, your epitaph to make, 162
Or whether doth my mind, being crowned with you, 228
Poor soul, the center of my sinful earth, 292
Say that thou didst forsake me for some fault, 178
Shall I compare thee to a summer's day? 36
Sin of self-love possesseth all mine eye 124
Since brass, nor stone, nor earth, nor boundless sea, 130
Since I left you, mine eye is in my mind, 226
So am I as the rich whose blessèd key 104
So are you to my thoughts as food to life, 150
So is it not with me as with that muse, 42
So now I have confessed that he is thine, 268
So oft have I invoked thee for my muse, 156
So shall I live, supposing thou art true, 186
Some glory in their birth, some in their skill, 182
Some say thy fault is youth, some wantonness, 192
Sweet love, renew thy force; be it not said 112
Take all my loves, my love; yea, take them all. 80
Th' expense of spirit in a waste of shame 258
That god forbid, that made me first your slave, 116

That thou art blamed shall not be thy defect, 140
That thou hast her it is not all my grief, 84
That time of year thou mayst in me behold 146
That you were once unkind befriends me now, 240
The forward violet thus did I chide: 198
The little love-god lying once asleep 308
The other two, slight air and purging fire, 90
Then hate me when thou wilt, if ever, now, 180
Then let not winter's ragged hand deface 12
They that have pow'r to hurt, and will do none, 188
Thine eyes I love, and they, as pitying me, 264
Those hours that with gentle work did frame 10
Those lines that I before have writ do lie, 230
Those lips that love's own hand did make 290
Those parts of thee that the world's eye doth view 138
Those pretty wrongs that liberty commits 82
Thou art as tyrannous, so as thou art, 262
Thou blind fool love, what dost thou to mine eyes, 274
Thus can my love excuse the slow offense 102
Thus is his cheek the map of days outworn, 136
Thy bosom is endearèd with all hearts 62
Thy gift, thy tables, are within my brain 244
Thy glass will show thee how thy beauties wear, 154
Tired with all these, for restful death I cry, 132
Tis better to be vile than vile esteemed, 242
To me, fair friend, you never can be old, 208
Two loves I have, of comfort and despair, 288
Unthrifty loveliness, why dost thou spend 8
Was it the proud full sail of his great verse, 172
Weary with toil, I haste me to my bed, 54
Were't ought to me I bore the canopy, 250
What is your substance, whereof are you made, 106
What potions have I drunk of siren tears, 238
What's in the brain that ink may character 216
When forty winters shall besiege thy brow 4
When I consider every thing that grows 30

When I do count the clock that tells the time, 24
When I have seen by time's fell hand defaced 128
When in disgrace with fortune and men's eyes 58
When in the chronicle of wasted time 212
When most I wink, then do mine eyes best see, 86
When my love swears that she is made of truth 276
When thou shalt be disposed to set me light 176
When to the sessions of sweet silent thought 60
Where art thou, Muse, that thou forget'st so long 200
Whilst I alone did call upon thy aid, 158
Who is it that says most, which can say more 168
Who will believe my verse in time to come 34
Whoever hath her wish, thou hast thy Will, 270
Why didst thou promise such a beauteous day 68
Why is my verse so barren of new pride, 152
Your love and pity doth th' impression fill 224

SPARKNOTES LITERATURE GUIDES

1984
The Adventures of Huckleberry Finn
The Adventures of Tom Sawyer
The Aeneid
All Quiet on the Western Front
And Then There Were None
Angela's Ashes
Animal Farm
Anna Karenina
Anne of Green Gables
Anthem
Antony and Cleopatra
Aristotle's Ethics
As I Lay Dying
As You Like It
Atlas Shrugged
The Autobiography of Malcolm X
The Awakening
The Bean Trees
The Bell Jar
Beloved
Beowulf
Billy Budd
Black Boy
Bless Me, Ultima
The Bluest Eye
Brave New World
The Brothers Karamazov
The Call of the Wild
Candide
The Canterbury Tales
Catch-22
The Catcher in the Rye
The Chocolate War
The Chosen
Cold Mountain
Cold Sassy Tree
The Color Purple
The Count of Monte Cristo
Crime and Punishment
The Crucible
Cry, the Beloved Country
Cyrano de Bergerac

David Copperfield
Death of a Salesman
The Death of Socrates
The Diary of a Young Girl
A Doll's House
Don Quixote
Dr. Faustus
Dr. Jekyll and Mr. Hyde
Dracula
Dune
East of Eden
Edith Hamilton's Mythology
Emma
Ethan Frome
Fahrenheit 451
Fallen Angels
A Farewell to Arms
Farewell to Manzanar
Flowers for Algernon
For Whom the Bell Tolls
The Fountainhead
Frankenstein
The Giver
The Glass Menagerie
Gone With the Wind
The Good Earth
The Grapes of Wrath
Great Expectations
The Great Gatsby
Greek Classics
Grendel
Gulliver's Travels
Hamlet
The Handmaid's Tale
Hard Times
Harry Potter and the Sorcerer's Stone
Heart of Darkness
Henry IV, Part I
Henry V
Hiroshima
The Hobbit
The House of Seven Gables
I Know Why the Caged Bird Sings
The Iliad
Inferno

Inherit the Wind
Invisible Man
Jane Eyre
Johnny Tremain
The Joy Luck Club
Julius Caesar
The Jungle
The Killer Angels
King Lear
The Last of the Mohicans
Les Miserables
A Lesson Before Dying
The Little Prince
Little Women
Lord of the Flies
The Lord of the Rings
Macbeth
Madame Bovary
A Man for All Seasons
The Mayor of Casterbridge
The Merchant of Venice
A Midsummer Night's Dream
Moby Dick
Much Ado About Nothing
My Antonia
Narrative of the Life of Frederick Douglass
Native Son
The New Testament
Night
Notes from Underground
The Odyssey
The Oedipus Plays
Of Mice and Men
The Old Man and the Sea
The Old Testament
Oliver Twist
The Once and Future King
One Day in the Life of Ivan Denisovich
One Flew Over the Cuckoo's Nest
One Hundred Years of Solitude
Othello
Our Town

The Outsiders
Paradise Lost
A Passage to India
The Pearl
The Picture of Dorian Gray
Poe's Short Stories
A Portrait of the Artist as a Young Man
Pride and Prejudice
The Prince
A Raisin in the Sun
The Red Badge of Courage
The Republic
Richard III
Robinson Crusoe
Romeo and Juliet
The Scarlet Letter
A Separate Peace
Silas Marner
Sir Gawain and the Green Knight
Slaughterhouse-Five
Snow Falling on Cedars
Song of Solomon
The Sound and the Fury
Steppenwolf
The Stranger
Streetcar Named Desire
The Sun Also Rises
A Tale of Two Cities
The Taming of the Shrew
The Tempest
Tess of the d'Ubervilles
The Things They Carried
Their Eyes Were Watching God
Things Fall Apart
To Kill a Mockingbird
To the Lighthouse
Treasure Island
Twelfth Night
Ulysses
Uncle Tom's Cabin
Walden
War and Peace
Wuthering Heights
A Yellow Raft in Blue Water

Notes

Notes

Notes

Notes